EFFECTIVE CHANGE
Twenty ways to make it happen

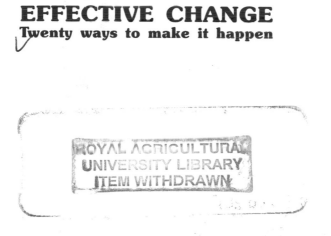

Andrew Leigh is a director of Maynard Leigh Associates, a Fellow of the IPD and author of a number of other IPD books on management, including *20 Ways to Manage Better* and *Persuasive Reports and Proposals*. He advises companies about management development particularly in the area of teams, leadership and coaching.

Mike Walters is head of human resources development with The Co-operative Bank plc. Prior to joining the bank, he spent a number of years as a principal consultant with ER Consultants, leading numerous major organisational change projects for private- and public-sector clients. His previous career includes a period as a development manager with the (former) Institute of Personnel Management (since 1994 the Institute of Personnel and Development), and human resource management roles for Shell and the BBC. Mike is author or co-author of several publications, including *Attitude and Opinion Surveys, Changing Culture* (both published by the IPD), and *Building the Responsive Organisation*. He is the editor of *The Performance Management Handbook*, also published by the IPD.

The Institute of Personnel and Development is the leading publisher of books and reports for personnel and training professionals, students, and for all those concerned with the effective management and development of people at work. For details of all our titles, please contact the Publishing Department:

tel. 0181-263 3387

fax 0181-263 3850

e-mail us on publish@ipd.co.uk

The catalogue of all IPD titles can be viewed on the IPD website:

http://www.ipd.co.uk

EFFECTIVE CHANGE
Twenty ways to make it happen

Andrew Leigh
and
Mike Walters

2nd edition

Institute of Personnel and Development

For my sister, Vivienne

First edition 1988
Reprinted 1991, 1994, 1997

Second edition 1998

Typeset by The Comp-Room, Aylesbury
Printed in Great Britain by the Cromwell Press, Trowbridge, Wiltshire

British Library Cataloguing in Publication Data
A catalogue record for this book is available from the British Library.

ISBN 0 852 92 741 X

INSTITUTE OF PERSONNEL
AND DEVELOPMENT

IPD House, Camp Road, London SW19 4UX
Tel: 0181 971 9000   Fax: 0181 263 3333
Registered office as above. Registered Charity No. 1038333
A company limited by guarantee. Registered in England No. 2931892

Contents

Acknowledgements

I should like to thank the following: Dr Jean Neumann of the Tavistock Institute of Human Relations who offered much appreciated encouragement and advice; John Nichol of the Work Research Unit; Bryan Stevens, Director of the Industrial Participation Association; *Community Care* magazine for permission to adapt material from two published articles of mine on Stress and Power; library staff of the Institute of Personnel and Development and also the London Borough of Croydon; the London Borough of Croydon for permission to use material relating to the social services department; Macmillan Publishing Company for a review copy of *Thriving on Chaos* by Tom Peters; William Collins Sons & Company for a review copy of *Odyssey* by John Sculley; Bantam Press for a review copy of *The Renewal Factor* by Robert Waterman, Jr; Matthew Reisz for suggesting this book; my own management team for never failing to remind me that writing about management is not the same as doing it; my wife Gillian for her ever constant support and my two sons, Aiden and Darion, who cheered from the sidelines.

Introduction by Andrew Leigh

If you are in management or leadership today, you are inescapably a change agent. Nobody avoids the pervasiveness of change in our fast-moving society and the abiding issue is how we can be proactive, rather than victims of its consequences.

Naturally with such an all-encompassing experience there is a plethora of advice available. Much is either contradictory or frankly rather banal. There is an understandable tendency amongst busy managers to conclude that, like riding a bicycle, you can hardly expect to know how to handle change through reading books.

What *Effective Change* tries to do is cut through the dense undergrowth and help you find your way through admittedly difficult terrain. After all, if it was easy to follow the path why would so much be written and talked about in respect of change management?

This new edition of *Effective Change* has the same intentions as the original published a decade ago, which is to be a practical resource to anyone wanting to manage or understand organisational change. So as well as descriptive material there are some well-tried tools and techniques that you can try out for yourself.

When the book was first published I had just completed over 16 years as a senior manager in the public sector and was setting up my own management development consultancy. The text contained many classic or current stories of successful management initiatives which, I am delighted to say, have stood the test of time and remain very stimulating.

Yet there are also a number of areas where fresh approaches are now relevant. I have long wanted to update this publication, but building a business leaves little room for such extra-curricular activity. I was therefore enormously grateful when Mike Walters, himself a highly experienced consultant and manager, kindly agreed to bring his own perspectives and insights to this revised second edition. He has written three powerful new chapters on communications, project management techniques for driving through change, and facilitation tools other than force-field analysis. He has also introduced substantial additional sections on:

- leadership styles for today's far more diverse workforces

- business ethics and values

- overcoming individual resistance to change, and

- techniques for surveying employee attitudes and concerns.

If after reading this new edition of *Effective Change* you feel it has been helpful, then both the reader and the joint authors can feel satisfied. If it makes you want to find out still more, then we have all had a success.

1 Models

Change has always been big business. Most societies have faced it in some form, whether political, military, social, economic or technological. How to make things happen, how to cope with change, live with it, love it and ultimately make use of it has fascinated humankind for millennia.

Despite its prevalence, however, enormous energy goes into resisting change. So what's new? Several factors are causing a rethink about how managers should handle change. First, there is the realisation that organisational change is here to stay. We must stop opposing it and, like a judo expert, turn it to our advantage.

Figure 1
The goals managers seek

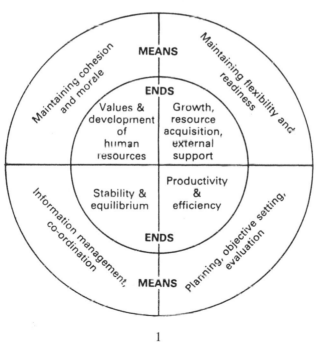

1

Stability was once a central management goal. The demand was for organisations in which you could predict and control events, organisations in which it was 'safe' to work. A manager worrying about stability becomes fixated on information and control. Harold Geneen, the legendary boss of ITT, epitomised this attitude. He had an astounding grasp of information. Nightly he left the office clutching several brief cases bulging with reports and accounts. Next day he returned, having read them all.

Yet stability is only one type of goal. Equally relevant are those shown in Figure 1. Organisations wanting to survive and grow must abandon the stifling effects of demanding certainty, predictability and minimal risk. Nor can they opt solely for growth, productivity or simply developing human assets.

Competing goals force us to accept that moving towards one may take us away from another. Hence we must be willing to accept a certain amount of instability. Taking this view to its logical conclusion the American efficiency specialist Tom Peters argues that 'success will come to those who love chaos – constant change, not those who attempt to eliminate it.'

Pace of change

The second factor that has forced a rethink in handling change is the accelerating pace of change. The impact has become so noticeable that in the 1970s Alvin Toffler dubbed it 'Future Shock' and people have been writing, researching and commenting on it ever since. What are

Box 1

Technological factors that will influence change
1   Genetic engineering
2   Electronic office
3   Automotive technology
4   Communications
5   Construction advances
6   Space technology
7   Energy
8   Military aerospace technology
9   Transportation
10   Medical technology
11   Robotics
12   New materials
13   Measurement tools
14   Personal computers and networks
15   Artificial intelligence

these changes? They are varied and not easily summarised except with rather unhelpful headings like political, social, demographic, economic forces.

If we analyse them in more detail, we begin to realise what is happening around us. Some of the technology factors are shown in Box 1. There are also complex social forces at work. Box 2 shows some 18 aspects of traditional life undergoing shifts likely to affect the environment in which organisations must exist. The dizzy pace of changes in company fortunes are more than enough to produce executive paranoia and stress. Only a few short years after quoting their examples of long-term success stories, the authors of *In Search of Excellence* were explaining the adverse changes in fortunes of many of the original companies.

The changes that many organisations have had to face in a decade or so have been stunningly symbolised by the motor industry and its suppliers, but there are also plenty of examples in other fields, ranging from computers to mining, from local government to hotels. Today's manager knows that we are living in a period of rapid change, and today's businessman does not need convincing of the necessity for responding to that change. As one European consultancy firm has pointed out:

> much that is written is like feeding horror stories to someone who is already living in a nightmare. It confirms his fears and strengthens his resolve to change but offers little practical help in the way of signposts or guidelines.

Many managers, unsure how to respond, become obsessed with structures, centralisation versus decentralisation, quality of work programmes, revamping incentive systems, new personnel systems and so on. Once it hardly mattered if change was approached in such a narrow way as there was scope to recover from any major mistakes. But for the foreseeable future the climate is turbulent and stressful, and the price of large-scale failure has become unacceptably high.

Considering the mass of contradictory advice from often highly credible and respectable sources, it is no wonder that many managers believe that learning to handle change constructively only comes from hard won experience (see Box 3). Yet it is possible to make some sense of what seems to work. A useful starting point is to have a model of organisational change which you can personally use, a mind map which is not confined to textbooks and management courses.

There is no universal model or framework of organisational change, however, and each manager must arrive at their own by an amalgam of personal values, hunches, attitudes, beliefs and perceptions. Models are

Box 2

Emerging social changes

Traditional	Emerging
(1) Quality of life and quality of work life seen primarily in economic terms.	— Expanded quality of life and quality of working life values with growing emphasis on personal growth, self realisation, fit with social/physical environment.
(2) Long-term results orientation towards rewards (from savings, promotion, superannuation, rewards in heaven).	— Short-term rewards, hedonistic orientation – live now, buy now, pay later, enjoy immediate satisfaction.
(3) 'Protestant work ethic' – unquestioning acceptance of hard work, thrift – belief in free, capitalistic enterprise.	— Conditional work ethic depending on job security, interest challenge, growth opportunities – belief in controlled markets, cargo-cult, socialism.
(4) Accepted hierarchy of loyalties and responsibility – to God, country, family, class group.	— Variable loyalties and unclear responsibility; new hierarchy in descending order may be self, family, class group, country, God.
(5) Sanctity of property ownership, exploitative materialism, little concern for environment/ecology.	— Shift to rights of use and access to resources, awareness of societal ownership and ecological/ environmental impacts.
(6) Relative community of interests among interdependent producer groups, along with rugged competitive individualism.	— Growing adversarial social group rivalries and competitions for special treatment, along with growing interdependence and collaboration within groups.
(7) Declining union membership among blue collar workers.	— Growing white collar and professional unionism.
(8) Acceptance of selected drugs (tobacco, alcohol).	— Acceptance of drug abuse as normal (hard drugs, drunkenness), decline in tobacco.
(9) Respect for authority of position and hierarchical decisions, trust in government.	— Growing disrespect for authority of position and government, growing respect for demonstrative expertise and desire for social consensus, participation in decision-making.
(10) Acceptance of the *status quo*, conformity to established social norms, stability and routines.	— Acceptance of dissent, tolerance to non-conformity of social norms, innovations, change, flexibility.

(11) Acceptance of rigid moral and ethical principles of established religions.	— Relativism and more relaxed situation-based ethics and morals – gap between religious principles and practice.
(12) Acceptance of male dominance and double standards.	— Growing freedom of women, and toward economic, sexual, social equality.
(13) Racial cultural intolerance	— Greater acceptance of multi-racial, multi-cultural factors as enriching every society.
(14) Acceptance of paternalistic, but fair government and business, and of market mechanisms.	— Growing resentment and lack of trust, along with increasing demands on government and business.
(15) The individual as the basic unit and goal for social change – all men are equal.	— Social groups as the basic units which advance us as individuals – 'all men are equal but some are more equal than others'.
(16) Concern and resentment toward injustice (eg unemployment).	— Apathy, resignation, rationalisation for injustice (eg unemployed are mainly dole dodgers), with the emergence of a semi-permanent class of jobless persons.
(17) A relatively even distribution of age cohorts in nuclear families.	— Rapidly ageing populations, with shift to non-nuclear families and isolation of oldies.
(18) Education mainly of young people, creating realistic expectancies.	— More education of young people and continuing education of adults, creating unrealistic expectations.

Source: 'Developing managers for social change', P Helius, *Journal of Management Development,* Vol 3, No 1, 1984

a mindset for thinking about something clearly. They stimulate more creative ways of tackling where, when and how to intervene to make things happen.

From here to there

The simplest framework for thinking about the change process appears in Figure 2 in which diagnosis of the need for change leads on to planning and eventually to interventions. The latter lead to more problems and opportunities producing a new round of diagnosis, planning and interventions. In various forms this model will be used throughout this book.

We can view change from several angles. The most personal is how

Box 3

Conflicting advice about change	
Analyse the need for change thoroughly	Don't bother! Organisations are too complex to justify the effort
Don't rush into action. Be more reflective about the likely impact of change	Have a bias for action; beware of the paralysis of analysis; action precipitates change
We know little about the true levers of change	We know quite a lot! Research has uncovered the essential change process and how to make it happen
Resistance to change is bad	Resistance is functional and should be welcomed
When you have made a big change, evaluate before continuing	Maintain the momentum; heap change on change to get real results
Go to great lengths to tell people what changes you want	Avoid announcements; make changes quietly so they become established facts of life
Reactive management is bad	Reactive management is good
Managers should be highly pro-active	Managers are too prone to rush into action
Good managers do not need to use power relationships to achieve change	Effective managers use power relationships to foster change
Stability should follow from a major change effort	Stability is unattainable and undesirable
React to the environment to avoid organisational obsolescence	Act on the environment and transform it
Treat the organisation as a giant system – everything depends on everything else	Treat the organisation as merely loosely linked subsystems
To manage change, manage the interdependencies	To manage change, promote individualism and personal autonomy
Change is best generated by good teamwork	Real change stems from rampant individualism and product or service champions
Go for evolutionary step-by-step change	Go for radical transformations
Participation reduces the power gap between managers and subordinates	Participation leaves the power gap unchanged, it merely links the needs of managers and subordinates

we as individuals must change ourselves, adapt and cope. Another angle, of particular interest to managers, is how organisations as a whole change. Excessive usage has turned the phrase 'organisational change' into a woolly concept, but at its simplest it is about moving a situation in the organisation from

HERE to .... THERE

Figure 2

A simplified view of the change process

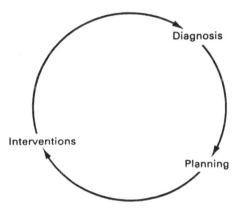

Change smashes the *status quo*, altering what happens in the enterprise. There are two main types of organisational change:

- strategic

- operational (day-to-day).

The first is highly distinctive and relates to the future direction of the organisation affecting one or more of the goals shown in Figure 1. Strategic change involves some major switch in what the organisation does and how it does it, and it usually takes place over months or years, rather than days or weeks.

Operational or day-to-day change, on the other hand, happens constantly. Managers are always either causing or responding to events which seldom in themselves amount to strategic change, although a succession of day-to-day events can accumulate into a significant shift. Another angle on operational change is that it is mainly opportunity change in which managers take advantage of situations to alter situations (see Chapter 8 on Planning).

The search for models

Missing from the mountainous pile of change literature, whether academic or autobiographical, are:

- a rigorously tested general model explaining how organisations work

- levers of change, which are generally known to work (validated).

There have been numerous attempts at capturing the essence of organisations, most of it descriptive rather than explanatory and prescriptive. Efforts to nail down the precise nature of the change process have been considerable and from the shaky foundations has come endless and often dubious advice on what does or does not work.

A prescriptive general theory of organisational change would be of limited use in daily affairs. What works for multinational or global companies would probably be useless to the small business or a local district council. This lack of a tested model is frustrating for busy managers who want workable ideas and tools. It partly explains the phenomenal success of best selling management guides based on a limited series of case studies, or highly personal accounts such as Chrysler boss Lee Iacocca's views on how to manage change. His entertaining autobiography pushed his popularity to cult status and there was even talk of him standing for President. After the dust settles from such literary wisdom doubts surface about the usability of the advice and the hunger for new panaceas is renewed.

The sheer messiness of handling organisational change and the absence of validated models and theories are no reasons for ignoring what can sometimes be helpful ways of looking at the task of handling change to produce constructive results.

The changing models

Models and theories are tools for making sense of the change process and are often spurned because they:

- do not accurately reflect the real world

- are incomplete and can encourage narrow thinking

- seldom offer detailed, validated guidance for action.

Despite these drawbacks they provide a rough framework, a mindset, within which to consider what results you want, how you might achieve them and the possible consequences of any actions. Apart from models of the change process itself there have been three important ways of viewing organisations that have influenced management thinking this century and hence how to achieve effective change: the traditional or classical model; the human relations model; and the systems model.

Traditional/classical model
The traditional/classical model sees organisations as machines, with layers of management, concerned mainly with mass production. Specialisation is triumphant. What counts are the buzz words of scheduling, planning, organising, monitoring, motivating, counselling and so on.

This model directs attention to spans of control and requires that people's authority matches their responsibilities. It has lost favour because it is rigid, predictable and does not reflect what actually occurs in real organisations.

Human relations model
Human relations models view organisations as living organisms with mutually connected and interdependent parts. Authority flows from below upwards, not from the top down. Groups have as much influence on change as the manager. This model is a reaction to the stark certainties of the mechanistic approach.

The buzz words for this model are managing groups, understanding the informal parts of the organisation, an emphasis on democratic leadership, flat hierarchies and team development.

Systems model
The vagueness of the human relations model only served to remind managers that their organisations were complicated. The systems model is a response to growing size and complexity. Confusion is made manageable by treating the organisation rather like a giant computer. Jargon from the computer field is used, such as inputs, outputs and various processes in between.

In a giant system everything is related to everything else. For managers, the message (summarised at the top of page 11) is:

Figure 3

A systems model

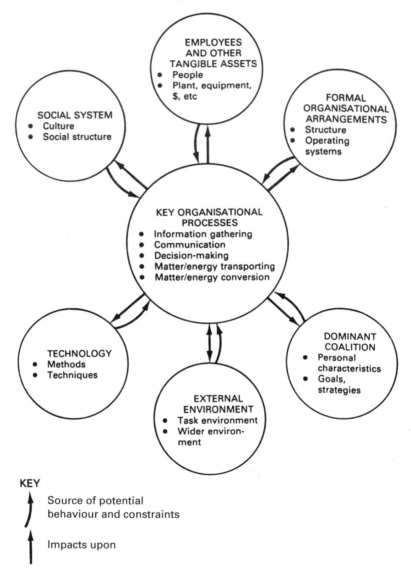

KEY

Source of potential
behaviour and constraints

Impacts upon

Source: J P Kotter, *Organizational Dynamics,* © 1978, Addison-Wesley Publishing
Company, Inc., Reading, Massachusetts. Reprinted with permission.

• To handle change well, you must understand the whole, then unravel how the bits fit together.

The buzz words for this model are openness in relationships, need for rationality, teamwork and cohesive groups, interdependence, and so on. A version of this model is shown in Figure 3. The systems model has had a significant impact on how managers handle change, particularly advanced technology. It has focused attention on what results the organisation wants and is achieving.

This model is losing its appeal because practical experience shows that mastering the interdependence of a giant, tightly linked system is beyond the skills of the majority of managers, no matter how well equipped they might be with analytical tools.

All three models have stimulated powerful suggestions for how managers should develop their organisations, such as Lickert's System 4 in which organisations move through various stages from authoritarian to participative; Blake's grid in which firms and managers move from concern only for production or only for people towards a more balanced approach; and McGregor's polarisation of the management approach into authoritarian or participative with his Theory X and Theory Y.

The loosely coupled system
From this battleground of models has come a more pragmatic view of the organisation. It is a realistic response to the extreme rate of change of our times.

Although the organisation is still seen as various subsystems these are almost independent and only loosely linked to create the whole. They are systems of action rather than geographical chunks of the enterprise. The systems model makes managers take a macro look at the organisation by expecting them to understand its parts by first understanding the whole. The loosely coupled model on the other hand asks managers to take a more micro view, expecting them to grasp the whole through understanding the parts.

This newer model accepts change and turbulence; despite their impact the entire system is bound together by shared values, sentiments and symbols. The manager is still concerned with interdependencies, but between different systems of action, not people. The main actor in this model is often the individual, not a group.

The buzz words for this model are decentralisation, devolution, smaller corporate headquarters, smaller business units, and the autonomy of individuals. A version of this model is shown in Figure 4. For senior managers interested in handling change the loosely coupled model has important implications. One of the main tasks of top

Figure 4

The renewal ring

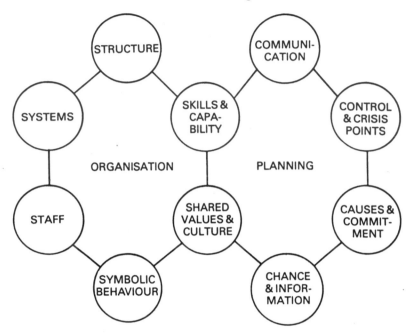

Source: The Renewal Factor, Waterman J. Jn, Bantam Press, 1988

management is managing the organisation's culture and values. Managers are concerned with developing an overall vision with which to inspire and direct the subsystems (see Chapter 3 on Vision and Values).

Teamwork is taken for granted. Individuals are not trapped by the group's boundaries. When the interests of the organisation demand it individuals act to transform and if necessary transcend the group. In this model the personal values which individual employees hold are important, not a minor irritation. What counts is how you promote the freedom of the individual to work with others for the benefit of the organisation. Thus personal autonomy has a central place in this particular model.

Strengthening the individual's role is a particular challenge for managers. It has been seen to work, for example, in abolishing quality inspectors and putting the responsibility where it belongs, with those actually doing the work. Widening the individual's role means tolerating

Figure 5

New skills managers need for handling change

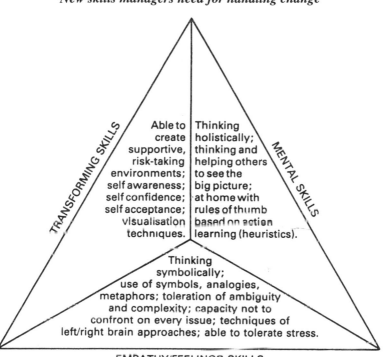

EMPATHY/FEELINGS SKILLS

ambiguity, independence, and an ability to deal with complexity. Consequently the management skills for handling change are different to those previously expected (see Figure 5). There is more emphasis on empathy and feelings, on transforming skills such as visualisation techniques and on certain types of mental abilities such as seeing the 'big picture' (see also Chapter 2 on Leadership).

Loosely coupled subsystems are an alternative to seeing change as occurring in a giant system which the manager must somehow learn to master. Instead, change is a developmental process in which **growth** and **direction** are the main issues – the model is going somewhere. Everyone is a change agent. The manager can be seen less as an analyst and more like a gardener tending a plant, watching and helping it grow in its own natural direction.

Using this model enables you to identify expectations about the future, both your own and the organisation's. 'Where are we going?' becomes a central issue along with 'how are we going to get there?'

Relevance

Perhaps you feel that viewing your organisation in this way is irrelevant and unrelated to practical use? Are you so sure? The revitalised role of the individual for example, can already be seen in job advertisements for those with leadership skills, in the major thrust by both the public and private sector to decentralise, eliminate large headquarters, in the search for product and service innovators and in the style of training that increasingly stresses concepts from this new model.

In Britain's public sector it can be seen for instance in the contracting out of certain services and the emergence of new relationships between various groups, as between:

- the council and central government departments

- the council and private tenderers

- the council and grant receiving bodies

- managers and subordinates

- managers and professionals

- professionals and those in receipt of their services

- one department and another.

In the loosely coupled model managers achieve change by influencing the subsystems, not the entire enterprise in one go. Since there are many subsystems it can be helpful to reduce these to manageable proportions as in the strategic rope (Figure 6) in which the organisation is simplified into three woven-together strands: technical, cultural, political.

As with a rope these strands are not easily distinguished from a distance. In achieving strategic change the management role is to unravel the strands and then work on one or more in depth; secondly to knit them together again so that change is implemented and made permanent. Integrating the strands is an ongoing management activity, not a once only event.

The strategic rope idea is also useful because it draws attention to a common tendency amongst practising managers to put their trust in a

Figure 6

Strands of the strategic rope

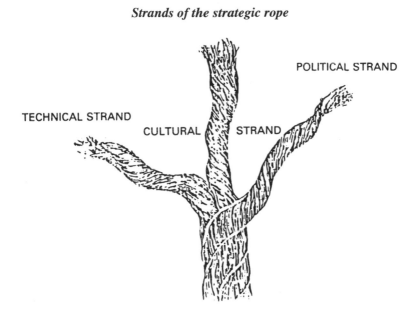

POLITICAL STRAND

TECHNICAL STRAND

CULTURAL STRAND

Figure 7

Strategic change model

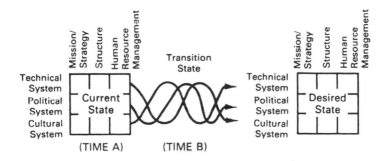

Source (of both charts): 'Essentials of strategic management', by Noel Tichey, *Journal of Business Strategy* (USA), Spring 1983

single way of achieving change. Regardless of the nature of the problem some managers will always restructure, others will always improve communications, whilst others will always alter how services or goods are produced.

To affect the three subsystems managers can use the tools of mission or strategy, structure, administrative and human resource procedures. Figure 7 shows Noel Tichey's strategic change model. It emphasises time, the movement from

HERE to .... THERE

In changing from one state to another the organisation passes through a separate transition phase. Whether it takes a long or short time to complete this phase the transition phase is distinctly different from the desired or end state.

This picture of change focuses our attention on a usually much neglected issue, namely 'what happens before we reach the end state?' Managing the transition state can be a complex task requiring considerable skill. Some managers are much better at initiating change and handling the transition stage than they are the results of the transformation. Some people prefer developing and creating while others enjoy consolidating and systematising.

GUIDELINES

- *Distinguish* between strategic and operational change.

- *Develop* a personal model of organisational change which you find helpful – not one confined to the textbooks and management courses.

- *Use* models to help stimulate and clarify thinking about change and the consequences.

- *Avoid* putting trust in one way of achieving change. Use the strategic rope concept of technical, cultural, political strands to consider how to tackle change.

- *Give* attention to the transition stage of change not merely the end state.

2 Leadership

When Tony Blair became leader of the Labour Party and subsequently prime minister, 'leadership' was one of the words used most frequently in describing his approach – not least by Mr Blair himself. He was determined to demonstrate a contrast with the widely held perception of the previous administration. In support of this, a computer search of newspaper reports shortly before the 1997 general election found countless references to 'leadership' in respect of Mr Blair and none relating to his predecessor. Rightly or wrongly, in the eyes of the public, Mr Blair, like Margaret Thatcher before him, was perceived as a 'leader'.

Objectively, though, it is difficult to see the exact nature of Blair's leadership. Certainly, he had introduced some significant changes in his own party, and had arguably shown courage and decisiveness in doing so. Nevertheless, his role till then had been to 'lead' an essentially democratic organisation, where ultimate decisions were made collectively. And, because his parliamentary role had been limited to leader of the opposition, he had not yet been able to take any genuine legislative or other governmental action.

Mr Blair's perceived 'leadership' qualities, therefore, were perhaps more about his style, approach and vision – his ability to define a context within which change could take place, within which goals and ideas could be enacted. There is little doubt that the concept of 'leadership' was one of the factors that influenced many who voted for him and his party in 1997. At a national level this echoes the description, by the management theorist Richard Beckhard, of the effective organisational leader as someone who enables employees to 'dream their own dreams'. It also reflects Warren Bennis's argument that too often we see the 'leader' as a hero or saviour who almost single-handedly brings about change.

What is leadership?

The simplest view of leadership is that it helps turn plans and decisions into action. Leadership is when:

people with certain motives and purposes mobilise resources so as to arouse, engage and satisfy the motives of followers.

This view reflects two principal leadership styles. The first is when leaders give followers what they want in exchange for things sought by the leader. The two parties may be seeking different results, and the relationship is thus transactional. The second leadership style is when leaders create situations in which the ends are desired by both leaders and followers. In this case the leaders raise the sights and aspirations of followers, and the relationship is thus a transforming one.

Virtually every research finding about leadership has been challenged or contradicted by other studies. Leadership is a sophisticated concept with as many different definitions as people who have attempted to define it (see Box 4).

Box 4

Different ways of looking at leadership

- A focus of group processes
- Personality and its effects
- The art of inducing compliance
- An exercise in influence
- Act or behaviour
- A form of persuasion
- Power relationship
- An instrument of goal achievement
- A way of defining an individual's role

The importance of leadership in achieving change stretches back to man's early history. It is therefore tempting to think that good leaders are born with, rather than create, the required qualities. Within organisations what has altered in recent years is first the realisation that leadership is not the exclusive preserve of the most senior manager, and secondly that today's leaders who make things happen are transformational, they revitalise entire organisations.

Everybody does it

Anybody can play a leadership role, depending on the local situation. During a major change effort, leadership may move around the organisation and be shared by many different people. In fact situations throw up leaders and leadership skills can certainly be learned both through work experience as well as carefully targeted training.

When a major US aerospace company which had diversified into a multinational concern, began trying to define what it meant by leadership, it gradually narrowed the field to:

- a clear sense of direction

- an ability to involve the whole organisation in clarifying that direction

- a willingness to encourage initiative and risk taking – and tolerance of failure

- a management style that empowers people to do the job without abdicating accountability

- an emphasis on teamwork.

To help to achieve these objectives the managers concluded that they needed to practise a range of skills including: creating and developing a shared vision; taking initiatives; empowering others; and gaining support in the organisation. This view of leadership stems from a highly practical need to turn a much misused concept into a management tool.

Transformational leadership reflects the realisation that most Western commercial organisations need to fundamentally rethink how they operate in order to survive in the face of fierce, at times brutal, competitive pressures. Public bodies too are facing similar demands for radical change. A local authority, for instance, asked to cut its spending by as much as 20 per cent is no longer in the cosy business of turning the wheels of the bureaucratic machine.

Transforming is a three act drama of recognising the need for revitalisation, creating a new vision and institutionalising changes. This is an endless cycle as shown in Figure 8.

The leadership tasks

From a combination of research and the practical experience of companies, we have a rough idea about what managerial leaders do to make things happen. These are shown in Box 5.

A clear sense of direction
Abraham Lincoln's administration was once criticised for stumbling

Figure 8

Transformational leadership: a three-act drama

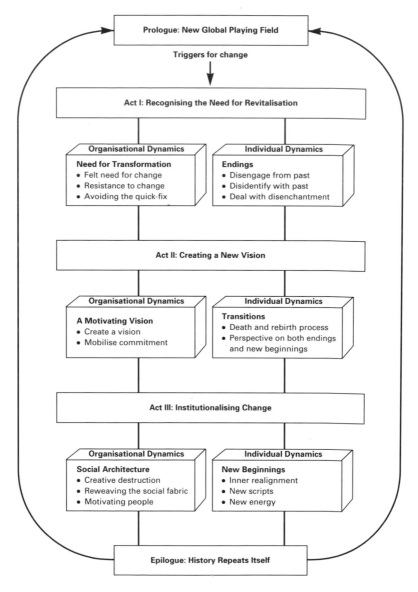

Source: *The Transformational Leader*, Tichey N, Devanra M, John Wiley, 1986

Box 5

> ### *How managers offer leadership*
>
> - **A clear sense of direction** (objectives)
>   - define goals
>   - involve whole organisation in clarifying that direction
>   - provide means for goal attainment
>   - maintain goal direction
>
> - **Values**
>   - engender core values
>   - pursue core values with total persistence and meticulous attention to details which help achieve this end
>   - constant interaction with employees to promote core values
>
> - **Excitement**
>   - engender this amongst employees
>
> - **Teamwork**
>   - emphasis on teamwork
>   - provide and maintain group structure
>   - facilitate group interactions
>   - maintain member satisfaction
>   - facilitate group task performance
>
> - **Accountability**
>   - empower people to do the job without abdicating accountability
>   - encourage initiative and risk taking
>   - tolerate failure

along. The president's reply was that while this might be true 'we are stumbling in the right direction'. A sense of direction, knowing 'where we are going' is what makes leaders attractive to followers. While managers often become stuck in a morass of objectives leaders are more concerned with a general direction than detailed targets.

Similarly managers are usually concerned with balancing operations in an organisation, relating to others according to their role. They are detached, impersonal, seek solutions acceptable as a compromise among conflicting values and identify totally with the organisation. By contrast managerial leaders focus on direction and matters of principle.

Leaders create new approaches and imagine new areas to explore. They relate to people more intuitively and in empathetic ways, moving to where opportunity and reward are high, and projecting ideas into images which excite people. Since the road to the final goal may be a long one, leaders also have the task of helping people to keep their sights on the end results and not become diverted to less relevant ones. They must be able to see and hold onto 'the big picture' (see also below).

Values

While it is possible that leadership and management may coincide, it is nevertheless true that effective managers are not always good leaders and successful leaders may sometimes be poor managers. What seems to set leaders apart from managers is found in the idea which the most effective leaders adopt in their work of changing their organisation:

- Managers do it right, leaders do what is right.

For example, one luxury-car manufacturer provided car rides for all employees as an exercise in leadership to highlight and enhance core values. Like children able to see beyond a playground for the first time, the upholsterers, for example, began marvelling at the engineering and the engineers at the comfort. 'It's beautiful, beautiful,' commented one upholstery fitter who did not even own a car.

Effective leadership pays meticulous attention to details that engender and show in practical ways the importance of core values. For example, a clothes manufacturer who declares that 'quality comes first' does little by his words to actually promote this value; removing every faulty item and asking all employees to attend a ritual burning of the defective goods would make the point more forcibly.

Leadership persistence in pursuing core values demands that these become a high priority for everyone. For example, the Adult Services Division of the London Borough of Croydon identified a core value as 'improving the quality of our services by actively involving users and their relatives'. To translate this statement into action senior management asked every team in the division to identify ways of doing this as part of setting their own annual objectives. Thus virtually all members of the staff were involved in discussing and planning the pursuit of the core value of involving users. It was further backed up with training support on how to be more helpful to users and their relatives.

Effective management leadership seeks to ensure a constant interaction with employees to promote core values. This goes beyond sending round notices or putting up posters. Management must be out and about communicating or modelling the importance of core values and hearing what obstacles there are to turning these values into a reality (see also Chapter 3 on Vision and Values).

Excitement

Change through leadership also means causing excitement, as the car-maker example above shows. Some years ago a leading computer company booked a football stadium to announce and praise the successes of its sales force. The huge electronic scoreboard flashed up the sales results of each individual salesman as they came running onto the pitch to cheers from the audience of employees, friends and relatives. Outrageous? Perhaps, yet employees of the company still talk about it to this day. Excitement keeps alive those values and goals that leaders want to pursue.

Teamwork

Most managers will affirm that they believe in teamwork; leaders actually achieve it. Sometimes this is done with team building skills. Occasionally, however, using teams stems from fear – people are forced to use teams as a defensive way of coping with anxiety or uncertainty. Effective leaders must model good behaviour by paying attention to teamwork in their own working group of senior managers (see Chapter 19 on Team-Building).

Accountability

Interest has been growing in recent years in how organisations can promote the employees' autonomy. This concern reflects the extent to which leadership has previously been relegated to a back seat in favour of the managerial role.

In managing change leaders hand over power in numerous ways. They accept that goals can only be achieved if people accept responsibility for taking initiatives. How far this approach permeates throughout the organisation depends on management style. A participating style will expect this accountability to go both wide and deep.

Leaders also refuse to become embroiled in areas of responsibility which rightly belong to their subordinates. By constantly asking 'why can't you deal with it?' leaders challenge their followers to assert themselves and maximise their own use of authority and accountability.

Leadership skills

Learning the various activities associated with the leadership of change does not depend solely on an inherited talent. It may often rely on being thoroughly tenacious about finding new ways to undertake key tasks.

Increasingly organisations are operating as groups of subsystems which are loosely connected, not as single systems in which managers must understand all the complicated interdependencies. In this loosely coupled system leadership demands rather different skills to those associated with more traditional models of the organisation (see Chapter 1 on Models).

If organisations are just a bunch of loosely linked subsystems whose connections are hard to understand, managers need leadership skills if they are to manage change adequately. These skills include:

- transforming

- ability to get things done

- ability to see the big picture

- ability to think clearly

- personal maturity.

Transforming skills

Across the industrial and commercial landscape we are seeing the emergence of a new breed of leader – the transformational leader. These people take on the responsibility for revitalising an organisation, defining the need for change, creating new visions and mobilising commitment to these visions. Ultimately they intend to transform the organisation. This kind of thinking demands new thinking about strategy, structure and people.

The ability to manage and relate to people is now widely seen as a core skill in managing change. There is a stress on combining right brained activity (thinking which is creative and intuitive) with left brained thinking (that which is systematic, logical and rational).

In tomorrow's organisations the recognition of the autonomy of the individual will have a central place in management thinking and action. Already there are clear signs that advanced organisations are recognising this in highly practical ways.

One well-known development, pioneered by the Xerox Corporation, has been the idea of networking, in which employees are encouraged to leave the payroll to establish their own organisation which directly serves the mother firm which guarantees a certain amount of paid work on regular contract. Transforming leadership is thus able to find ways to develop and supervise autonomous individuals rather than depend on exercising coercive or hierarchical power in the more traditional way.

Managers will have to develop such skills increasingly if they want to produce results. In practical terms it means that you as a manager may have to:

- *depend* less on your position in the hierarchy and more on your expertise, leadership and personality

- *pay* more attention to what a wider range of other people in the organisation think and say

- *adapt* easily to new information and situations

- *attend* more to your own and other people's intuition

- *place* more value on the creative, experimenting style of making things happen

- *rely* less on rules, systems, procedures and control and hence live with a greater degree of risk and uncertainty

- *recognise* the needs of followers to satisfy their higher needs of personal development, autonomy and self realisation.

Ability to get things done

Making things happen is what managing change is all about. Where the various subsystems are often only connected by fairly tenuous links, effective leadership of change stresses proactive, transforming skills. The individual manager is motivated by an inner drive.

To get things done requires a manager to be more than responsive to people and situations. It demands pragmatic common sense combined with a good knowledge of the organisation's principal aims. In practical terms it means that you as a manager may have to:

- *formulate* your own goals

- *evaluate* your own successes and failures with ruthless and sometimes painful honesty

- *seek* constantly to clarify and simplify aims so that the tasks to make them happen are clearly identified and allocated

- *go* beyond your own job boundaries and take an interest in events throughout the whole organisation

- *test* constantly whether proposed action is really achievable and desirable

- *keep* an eye on the 'bottom line' which may be profitability, quality of service, morale and so on.

Ability to see the big picture

Organisational change means influencing the technical, cultural and political elements of the enterprise (see opening chapter). In the process it is easy to lose sight of the overall picture of what is being attempted. Managers constantly have to resist becoming bogged down in activities which, on reflection, are not really central to core values and priority tasks.

Thus leadership of change requires managers to avoid becoming trapped in side issues, details, paper work or irrelevancies. In practical terms it means that you as a manager may have to:

- *develop* political and networking skills in which you learn to read the political and economic climate

- *look* outward beyond your own work area and the organisation itself

- *acquire* public relations skills, in particular learning how to handle the media

- *organise* how you spend your time and limited energy

- *maximise* delegation

- *build* yourself good channels of communication and systems for monitoring what is happening.

Ability to think clearly

It is no coincidence that in the last few years there has been a rush of books and publications and training courses offering to help managers think more clearly and creatively about their work. The quality of your leadership depends on the quality of your thinking.

In organisations which are constructed of separate sub systems with links of varying strengths, managers must be extremely clear about goals and responsibilities, and be able to think through what they are trying to achieve. Intuition, right brain activity and the concept of thinking laterally, all form part of the culture of change. There is less emphasis on managers mastering their environment and more on being able to ask 'what if?' questions.

Hence the leadership task is to demand information about likely outcomes, not simply to say 'this is what we are going to do', though of course it still considers assessments of risk and coping with uncertainty. In practical terms it means that you as a manager may have to:

- *focus* attention on defining clear aims

- *search* constantly for new ways of doing things

- *take* few plans or proposals for granted

- *develop* scenarios of possible outcomes and evaluate these systematically.

Personal maturity

Maturity can be defined as how far a person is willing and able to take responsibility for their own behaviour. The effectiveness of your leadership of the change effort will depend on two aspects of maturity: your own and that of your followers.

Follower maturity

Researchers Hersey and Blanchard have argued that maturity should only be considered in relation to a specific task. You cannot generalise and say an employee is 'mature or immature'. People bring different degrees of maturity to the tasks which they perform. Though age brings maturity in one sense, it does not guarantee that a person develops a mature personality.

An important conclusion from this view of maturity is that there is no one best way to influence people. The leadership style that you should adopt with an individual or group depends on their maturity. Management leadership behaviour can be classified into:

- *direction* or task behaviour
  How much direction you provide, for example telling people what to do, how to do it and when. In a small group, for instance, the tasks include: initiating; elaborating or clarifying; co-ordinating; summarising; and recording.

- *support* or relationship behaviour
  The extent of a two-way communication with your people, including active listening; offering supportive and facilitating behaviour. In a small group this would include encouraging; reducing tension; and gatekeeping.

A combination of task behaviour and relationship behaviour produces four specific leadership styles: telling, selling, participating and delegating.

In exercising leadership you choose an appropriate style which reflects your followers' level of maturity. The maturity of followers can be graded along a continuum. Thus, selecting an appropriate leadership style depends on the right combination of direction and support in relationship to the maturity of followers. To diagnose the style required you can use the curve shown in Figure 9.

Telling is appropriate for low maturity followers, selling should be used with followers who have a low to moderate maturity and participating is suitable for moderate to high maturity. Delegating is reserved for followers of high maturity. This approach, called Situational Leadership suggests that to offer leadership of the change effort you must:

- *assess* the maturity level of those you want to influence

- *consider* ways to help followers grow in their maturity as far as they are willing and able

- *adjust* your own behaviour appropriately.

Your maturity

Situational Leadership demands that managers develop a good insight into their own behaviour and thinking. First, because to make things happen you require the active, committed help of other people. By knowing your own strengths and weaknesses you can more easily decide what type of help you need.

Secondly, leading a major change effort is a demanding role, usually involving considerable interaction with other people. This too is made easier and more effective if you have insight into how you perform during such interactions.

Thirdly, self awareness enables you to respond better during change. If you know that you tend to avoid risk taking, have a tendency to procrastinate or demand too much information before making a decision, then you can find ways to deal with these traits. Continuous self evaluation is therefore a common feature of effective leaders of major change efforts. They are always mentally reviewing their own performance, seeking new ways to be more effective.

An aspect of maturity which is not tied to chronological age is the ability to cope with stress. Sometimes younger managers are better able to handle stresses than their older colleagues who may see too many angles on a situation or become over-committed to certain people, ideas or ways of working which are being challenged by the change effort. A leader who handles stress well is likely to be more effective than one who does not.

A mature personality in practical terms means that you as a manager may have to:

- *spend* time regularly assessing your own strengths and weaknesses

- *seek* help willingly to review your personal performance objectively

Figure 9

Leadership styles

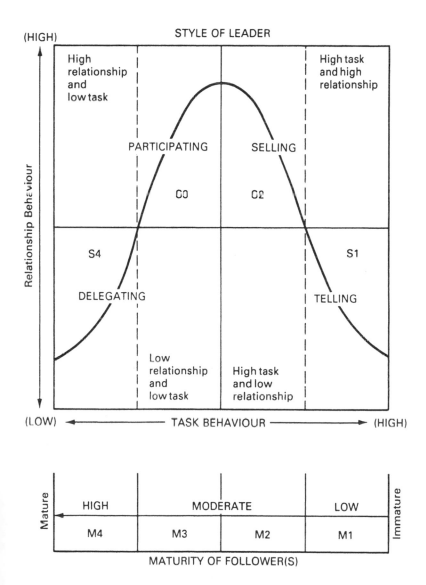

(HIGH)

STYLE OF LEADER

High relationship and low task

High task and high relationship

PARTICIPATING

SELLING

S3

S2

S4

S1

DELEGATING

TELLING

Low relationship and low task

High task and low relationship

Relationship Behaviour

(LOW) ◄──────── TASK BEHAVIOUR ────────► (HIGH)

Mature

HIGH | MODERATE | LOW

M4 | M3 | M2 | M1

Immature

MATURITY OF FOLLOWER(S)

- *create* a personal development programme, either within your organisation or outside it

- *acquire* a strong commitment to, or acceptance of, the values of the organisation; develop loyalty

- *learn* how to handle stress well.

The sign of a mature personality is that the manager copes well in a turbulent environment. Things get done despite both real and psychological barriers to change. The manager learns to live with and help others cope with complexity, uncertainty and ambiguity.

Finally, what do the successful leaders in organisations tend to be like? Box 6 shows the sort of qualities such people are likely to possess.

Box 6

Qualities of successful organisational leaders

- INTELLIGENCE – slightly higher than the average of their followers with an ability to analyse, comprehend situations and communicate effectively

- BREADTH AND MATURITY – generally possess broader interests than their followers; more shock proof, more mature emotionally and not over-elated by success or crushed by failure

- MOTIVATION AND DRIVE FOR ACHIEVEMENT – a strong personal need to keep achieving something; constantly seeking self realisation and creativity and work hard for satisfaction of inner drives rather than material rewards

- ATTITUDE TO PEOPLE – understand that they can only get their job done through others; develop a healthy respect for people and a skill in relating to them; employee orientated, approach problems in terms of people rather than technical aspects

- SPECIALIST KNOWLEDGE AND SKILLS – tend to have greater specialist knowledge and skill than followers in the particular specialisation of the group

---

Leaders of the future

The role of leaders in organisations continues to evolve, as the organisations face and respond to new challenges. The pace of change accelerates, external markets become increasingly competitive, organisational structures become ever more globalised and fragmented. The qualities discussed in this chapter are now increasingly critical as the old 'command and control' certainties are swept away. Against this background, what constitutes organisational leadership is likely to continue to undergo radical change.

Sally Helgesen, for example, has written extensively about how organisations can harness the diverse range of talents, styles and motivations potentially available in the workforce. She argues that leadership will become increasingly divorced from formal status or position. Helgesen cites the example of a senior engineer with the Intel Corporation, one of the earliest employees with the business, who holds no formal senior position, but who continues to influence the company's direction through his profound knowledge of the business and its requirements. Helgesen calls him a 'facilitator of power'.

Others have put forward the the idea of leadership as stewardship, in which the role is an essentially caring one. US commentator Gifford Pinchot suggests that, as businesses become increasingly fragmented and 'virtual', leadership needs to be effectively dispersed through the organisation. He identifies three phases through which the organisation may go while moving towards more fluid operations:

- organisation as hierarchy, where the key tool is delegation

- organisation as community, where the key tools are worthwhile vision and values, a gift economy

- organisation as economy, where the key tools are free intraprise, education and effective leadership of core businesses.

Pinchot envisages the organisations of the future as, in effect, mini-economies where the leader's role is to co-ordinate an internal free market (Pinchot's 'intraprise'). He argues: 'The new organisations will be pluralistic to the core, preferring conflict between competing points of view and the struggle of competing suppliers to the illusory security of bureaucratic command'.

Pinchot's vision may embody an extreme conception of the organisational free-market, but many of the elements he describes will already be in place – the restructuring of businesses into profit centres, the establishment of strategic business units to interface with the outside market, the growing use of outsourcing and managed services, the development of internal contracts and service level agreements. All of these are steps towards Pinchot's organisation as economy. In this context the role of the leader continues to change. The emphasis on moving increasingly away from 'hard' power relationships towards 'softer' skills of visioning, delegation and influencing.

Change and stakeholders

This fragmentation of the traditional organisation also reflects growing awareness that organisations and businesses cannot operate in isolation, but, as we discuss in Chapter 3, increasingly need to take account of the interests and expectations of the different groups with which they interact. The key principle is that corporate longevity (as opposed to rapid short-term profit) is more likely to be delivered through a balanced focus on all key stakeholders than through a one-dimensional concern with shareholder value.

Although these approaches so far remain relatively undeveloped, the key principles appear to be sound. After all, traditional financial measures of business performance are essentially retrospective and one-dimensional – they tell us how well the business has performed, but not why it has performed well or, except through crude extrapolation, how well it is likely to perform in the future. By contrast, measures such as customer or employee satisfaction, alongside measures of factors such as new product development, market share, brand perception and so on, are likely to provide us with a much better understanding of the organisation's capability. At the same time, by seeking greater involvement of key parties, such as customers, staff and suppliers, we are more likely to develop organisational solutions which will enhance our performance across these various areas.

For the change leader, this implies an increasingly multi-dimensional approach to change management. If we are managing an organisation's restructuring, for example, it is essential that we take account of the potential impact on all those involved. This does not mean that the organisation avoids tough business or operational decisions, but it does mean that, at all times, consideration should be given to factors such as customer service or employee satisfaction. For example, a decision to centralise all our customer interfaces into a single call-centre operation may make apparently sound financial sense in that it reduces our operating costs, but these savings may in the longer term be outweighed by the potentially negative impact on, say, levels of customer service or employee satisfaction.

This implies that, in planning and managing change, the leader has to take a multi-dimensional view of these various factors. This may include:

- seeking the views of the different groups in planning change

- measuring ongoing performance in terms of its impact on the different groups

- ensuring that the perceived financial benefits of the proposed change are not outweighed by less tangible (but perhaps ultimately more significant) impact on key stakeholders

- ensuring that the perceived long-term benefits of the change are not outweighed by the immediate impact of the changes on particular groups.

This last point is particularly critical. It is not uncommon for change leaders to assume that, in effect, the end justifies the means – 'This is going to save the company half a million a year, so we'll have to put up with some job losses or customer complaints while we're doing it.' This may be a legitimate business equation, but – even if we consider these issues in purely economic terms – it is easy to underestimate the negative impact on key stakeholders. We may never regain the customer who went off to our competitors because our service declined while we were concentrating on managing the changes. We may never recapture the staff trust and commitment which were lost because we handled the changes with excessive brutality or insensitivity. The effective change leader takes account of all these factors, and applies comprehensive and balanced measures to both the ongoing and the ultimate impact of change.

Change through partnership

This need for an 'inclusive' approach to change becomes even more pertinent as our traditional notions of the organisation become increasingly fragmented. In a growing number of organisations, traditional in-house operations are being 'unbundled' into external structures. At the same time, conversely, a growing number of innovative partnerships are being established to deliver new types of products or services. Companies such as Benetton have grown rapidly by developing a 'virtual' supply chain of external suppliers and franchised retail outlets. Virgin, similarly, has focused on marketing its distinctive brand across services as diverse as airlines, retailing, music, railways and financial services by forging alliances with appropriate partners. Even in the public sector, we have seen an increasing growth of cross-disciplinary partnerships to develop or deliver comprehensive public services – for example, in response to the demands of the Government's Single Regeneration Budget.

In this context, the leader's role in developing and communicating a shared vision becomes even more critical. The leader may be required to identify and reconcile conflicting aspirations or agendas among the different interest groups, and to find increasingly creative ways of establishing a shared direction which all parties can accept. In this environment, the successful leader will need effectively to balance compromise with clear direction. For the manager faced with delivering change through partnership, the leadership process is likely to include:

- ensuring clarity about the relative contribution, roles and influence of all the parties involved in the partnership. For example, who are the critical players? What are the potential implications of particular parties participating or not participating? Have we established an appropriate grouping, or are there some further parties who need to be involved?

- investing significant time and energy in ensuring full understanding of the interests, aspirations and expectations of all key parties. For example, do we fully understand why they are involved? What do they expect to receive from their participation? How much divergence is there in the goals or expectations of the various parties?

- developing a clear and common vision which all parties can accept. For example, what is the 'ideal' aim of the partnership? To what extent do the various participants 'buy in' to this ideal aim? Do we need to compromise the ideal in order to ensure the involvement of particular key players?

- implementing leadership styles to match the expectations and maturity of the various participants. In terms of Situational Leadership, for example, how mature are the different groups? What styles may we need to adopt to achieve results in each case? What is the nature of the power relationship between the leader and the different groups of followers?

This last point is particularly critical in leading change through partnerships. Although the leader in a traditional organisational structure may need to adopt differing styles at different times, the culture and nature of the organisation will generally dictate that one style is more appropriate (even though, as we have seen, this may require development as followers become more mature in their response to the activities involved). In a more fragmented or partnership arrangement, leaders may well have to become 'quick change artists', adopting different styles with different groups, shifting through the spectrum of leadership styles as they interact with different groups. Overall, leaders need to learn to be much more flexible, with the capacity to switch from, say, 'telling' to 'delegating' almost instantly as they handle different groups. In support of this, the leader requires ever more sophisticated skill in understanding his or her own strengths and weaknesses, and in quickly assessing the maturity of the different groups.

Leadership and diversity

Alongside this growing fragmentation of the traditional organisation, managers are in any case finding that, across all aspects of organisational life, they are required to lead and co-ordinate an increasingly diverse workforce, which in turn displays highly disparate qualities, expectations and motivations. In structural terms, for example, it may be necessary to deliver results, not merely through an established team of permanent employees, but also through fluid or cross-functional teams, through external consultants, external suppliers, franchisees, outsourced staff, and countless other 'strategic partnerships'. At the same time, increasing social change and mobility means that the overall profile of these various groups is likely to be changing. Although progress remains slow, for example, we are finally beginning to see a growing number of women entering senior management and other key organisational positions, including those in professions that have been traditionally male-dominated. In the same way, we are beginning to see individuals from highly diverse cultural backgrounds entering areas of society which have traditionally been largely white and middle-class.

It is probably too early to assess the full implications of these changes, many of which unfortunately still remain embryonic. Nevertheless, we can expect few of our current certainties to remain intact. As a minimum, we can be sure that these diverse groups will bring their own perceptions and perspectives, and will challenge many of our traditional ways of thinking – for example, about organisational power relationships, about career development and personal aspirations, about notions of organisational loyalty and commitment, about requirements for reward and recognition, and about overall values and beliefs.

This is not the place to debate the full implication of these emerging changes. However, it is clear that they will place increasing demands on the change-leader, requiring:

- the capacity to explore, understand and respond to the differing interests or expectations

- a willingness to abandon old assumptions or ways of thinking if these appear inappropriate to the emerging needs of followers

- the ability to communicate change goals or rationales in language and terms that are meaningful to all those involved

- above all, the capability and will to take on board the different perspectives and contributions of those involved, and to synthesise these differences into more effective and multi-dimensional solutions.

This last characteristic is likely to be the key determinant of the leader's success or failure in this changing environment. It is probable that, if we can effectively harness them, these diverse perspectives will enable us to develop change methods and outcomes which are more effective than ever before – not least because it is likely that those involved in delivering change will become more representative of those who will be affected by it.

Leadership and globalism

In addition to the growing diversity of organisational workforces, further diversity in leadership styles will doubtless emerge from the growing globalisation of business and markets. Charles Hampden-Turner and Fons Trompenaars, through their empirical research into national business cultures, have pointed out that many of our assumptions about the nature of management, of business and even of capitalism itself actually reflect relatively localised national cultures and characteristics. Factors which we have taken as management 'givens' may actually face significant challenge when they are opened up to more global perspectives.

This has become increasingly evident in recent years through our growing exposure to, for example, American or Japanese styles of management, but Hampden-Turner and Trompenaars point out that there are significant differences in values even within European nations. To take just one illustrative example, they argue that Scandinavian countries tend to be more comfortable operating at the 'delegation' end of the Situational Leadership spectrum. They suggest, for instance, that it is not coincidence that many Swedish companies – Asea Brown Boveri, IKEA, SAS, Volvo – are characterised by innovative management styles, since their studies suggest that Swedes are much more comfortable than many other cultures with concepts such as delegation, management responsibility, and taking a long-term view. Goran Carstedt of IKEA is quoted:

'If you believe in people and their latent capabilities, then the more authority you "give away" to them, the more you get back in ideas and initiatives even you did not foresee. We believe in radical decentralisation, in pushing authority down to the level where those dealing directly with customers have the freedom to exercise it.'

We are all operating in an increasingly global economy – whether as managers, employees or simply as consumers – and this diversity of attitudes and values is becoming ever more apparent. Hampden-Turner and Trompenaars argue not that particular values or styles are better or worse, but that different styles lend themselves more effectively to different types of business or production, and that this in turn constrains or enhances a nation's ability to compete in a developing economy.

In organisational terms, therefore, our long-term ability to handle change in an increasingly global economy is likely to depend on our ability to harness diversity, building on the most effective elements of each culture. This in turn may mean developing a style of leadership which facilitates continuing interaction across the business, building on and disseminating successful elements. Peter Senge, who introduced the concept of the learning organisation, identifies a critical need role for leadership in the future:

> Internal networkers or community builders, the 'seed carriers' of the new culture, who can move freely about the organisation to find those who are predisposed to bringing about change, help out in organisational experiments, and aid in the diffusion of new learnings.

This last role is likely to be an increasingly critical leadership requirement in the organisation of the future, particularly for those operating on a global or virtual basis. In Texas Instruments, for example, the transfer or secondment of key managers across national boundaries was seen as a key element of successful cultural and change management, enabling the company to draw on the full diversity of contribution made by its global workforce – helping them, in the words of one manager, to 'walk in each other's moccasins'.

GUIDELINES

- *Create* and protect core values

- *Persist* in pursuing core values

- *Seek* constant interaction with employees to promote core values

- *Engender* excitement

- *Rely* less on your position in the hierarchy and more on your expertise, leadership and personality

- *Listen* to what a wide range of other people in the organisation think and say

- *Respond* willingly to new information and situations

- *Value* your own and other people's intuition

- *Support* the creative, experimenting style of making things happen

- *Depend* less on rules, systems, and procedures and more on creativity, flair and a sense of direction

- *Evaluate* constantly your own successes and failures

- *Look* beyond your own job boundaries; take an interest in events throughout the organisation

- *Test* constantly whether proposed action is really achievable and desirable

- *Develop* public relations skills, in particular learning how to handle the media

- *Organise* how you spend your time and limited energy

- *Maximise* delegation

- *Build* good channels of communication and systems for monitoring what is happening

- *Seek* new ways of doing things

- *Take* few plans or proposals for granted

- *Create* scenarios of possible outcomes and evaluate these systematically

- *Assess* the maturity level of those you want to influence

- *Help* followers grow in their maturity as far as they are willing and able

- *Devise* a personal development programme, either within your organisation or outside it

- *Learn* to handle stress well

- *Take* a multi-dimensional view of the likely impact of change, reviewing the financial and other impacts on all the groups which might be affected, such as employees, customers or suppliers

- *Aim* to identify and reconcile conflicting aspirations or agendas among different interest groups, and seek creative ways of establishing a shared direction

- *Adopt* different styles with different groups, as appropriate, shifting through the spectrum of leadership styles

- *Be* willing to abandon old assumptions or ways of thinking if these appear inappropriate to the emerging needs of your followers

- *Seek* to communicate change goals or rationales in language and terms that are meaningful to all those involved.

3   Vision and values

In the early 1990s, the Co-operative Bank was performing poorly. Its financial performance was unsatisfactory, as the Bank struggled with the impact of the recession. Staff morale was low, and employees perceived the organisation as a 'poor relation' of the other major high-street clearing banks – trying to compete on the same basis, but on a much smaller scale with limited resources and capability. The future looked bleak.

Nevertheless, the Bank had a remarkable history. It had been founded in 1872 as part of the Co-operative Wholesale Society and had grown with the success of the Co-operative Movement through the twentieth century. Although small in comparison with its direct competitors it had a track-record of successful innovation in products and services. Above all, it had a distinct set of values, drawn from the principles of the Co-operative Movement, which influenced its approach to business and management.

Throughout the early 1990s, the Bank responded to its business challenges, not by abandoning or changing its core values, but by building on them to create a modern and vibrant new culture and image. For the first time the Bank began actively to promote its values, establishing a formal 'ethical stance' to its banking and investment policies developed through detailed consultation with its customers. With this ethical stance at its heart, the Bank created a distinctive new brand and corporate image, creating a market niche for itself which none of its competitors could easily duplicate.

The impact of this on the business has been dramatic. In recent years, the Bank has made record profits, year on year. Market awareness of the Bank is high and extremely positive. Even more significant, staff commitment has risen dramatically, with well over 90 per cent of employees declaring themselves proud to work for the organisation. For these staff the Bank is no longer a poor relation of its larger competitors but is a distinctive and highly effective business in its own right, which continues to innovate both in its products and services and in its overall approach to business. The Co-operative Bank totally transformed itself and its prospects because it had an existing set of values and beliefs which it placed at the heart of its continuing development. It developed and sustained an ultimately influential picture of what it was about and what it might become.

Creating a vision nails our colours to the mast. We state what the preferred future would look like. Vision channels our deepest values into the workplace; it is a word picture of how we see our values working. What makes organisations tick is not products, strategies or technology, it is people who are motivated by ideas, hopes and aspirations. These must be graspable by everyone – the vision must be easily shared. Managers become less concerned with manipulating things and people and more with manipulating ideas and concepts.

Vision does not replace the need for rational, analytical methods such as budgeting, reporting, control systems, objective setting and other quantitative measures. These are all necessary for running organisations. They are, however, capable of stifling innovation, creativity and the ability to drop existing plans and develop entirely new directions and achievements. Vision is closely connected to leadership which supplies and translates it into ways of making it a reality.

These days most managers have heard about vision and vision building and there is a danger that it will soon be relegated to the list of management techniques 'we tried and which did not work'. Perhaps more than any other aspect of achieving change, vision demands persistence and single-mindedness which must withstand sometimes outrageous pressures and temptations. The call for compromise, to abandon principles, to go for the easy fix are like the siren voices which Ulysses blocked out with wax in the ears. Equally the ability to modify the vision, altering it to fit new opportunities, is also important in keeping it alive.

Making it happen

Setting the vision apart from all the other words and documents jostling for attention is that it:

- expresses ideals

- inspires

- provides core values – against which plans, actions, and decisions can be judged

- does not define exactly how the end result will be achieved

- is understandable by absolutely everyone

- is what top management live by.

Vision is therefore a sincere expression of what we want. Unlike goals or objectives it is not precise. It is a licence to dare, to be better despite inertia and blockages. It mobilises people around what is not yet experienced.

In contrast to a mission statement, which says what kind of business we are in or compares our ranking against competitors, vision aims to capture our imagination and 'turn us on'. It will not contain numbers, complicated words, too many sentences, or be forgettable.

- Vision is about *values* – or what really matters.

- Mission is about *purpose* – or what business we are in.

- Objectives are about *strategy* – or how we will get there.

How do visions work? They make explicit what people want to do anyway, which is why they are so closely tied to good leadership. Leaders articulate what followers want, then show how to make it happen. Through visions managers who are leaders influence an organisation's norms which decide how change will be received and managed. Norms are hidden values which are in the areas shown in Box 7.

Vision affects change when the values which it represents start permeating people's daily behaviour. That is why vision has to be lofty, and try to inspire. If people do not feel inwardly drawn to it vision will make no impact, regardless of exhortation, monitoring or training.

Box 7

Where norms – the hidden values – are found

- Organisational and personal pride
- Performance and excellence
- Teamwork and communication
- Leadership and supervision
- Profitability and cost effectiveness
- Colleague relationships
- Customer and consumer relations
- Honesty and security
- Training and development
- Innovation and change

Building a vision statement

There are not 20 easy ways to build a vision. Creating one is a personal experience even if that occurs within a group. Because vision comes from within, developing it is a creative act. If you are going to live by a creed it cannot be produced by the marketing department or a committee of 'experts'. A vision statement is usually written down and built from core values such as those shown in Box 8.

Box 8

Some core values that may guide the vision

- We care about keeping our customers satisfied
- Everyone has the right to disagree
- We listen to what customers say
- We accept that success means tolerating failures
- What we say we will mean
- Being a manager is about supporting one's staff
- We believe in initiative and risk taking
- Quality comes first
- Value each employee as an individual

It takes time to identify these values. It is important to avoid producing slick slogans that have no gut feel and in which no one apart from the top management can really believe. You will know when you have anything approaching a vision statement if you and lots of other people agree that what it represents goes beyond an aim and should become a crusade. Crusades require zealots.

Developing a vision is messy, it evolves from past experience, making lists, talking with other people, encouraging people to participate in the task, chatting about what matters, what brought you into this line of work, scribbling on flipcharts, asking what people think. If you do this and identify some core values you may eventually be able to convert them into a statement which spells out the vision.

Values exercise

Since values underpin the vision you may find it helpful to conduct a values exercise with colleagues. There is nothing particularly demanding in organising this exercise and it does not need a consultant or trainer to do it. It is fun and can be both revealing and stimulating. The purpose is to discover how far you all share the same set of values and, if so, whether these can then be refined into a vision statement. To conduct the values exercise you need the items shown in Box 9.

The session starts with you or the senior manager responsible for the work group explaining about the importance of vision and values. Alternatively, give everyone a copy of the material below, down to the start of the description of the values exercise.

Box 9

Tools for a values exercise

Flipchart paper

One or more sets of 20–30 stiff cards measuring 3″ by 8″ on which are written core values (see below)

Blu-Tack™ and felt marker pens

One or more quiet rooms, preferably away from the normal workplace

Some core values for use in the exercise

Accountable	Planned
Achieving	Profit driven
Action minded	Quality first
Adaptable	Respectful
Approachable	Responsible
Caring	Responsive
Close to the customer	Rewarding
Competitive	Risk-taking
Excellence	Safe
Experimental	Sharing
Fair	Trusting
Friendly	Truthful
Fun	Useful
Innovative	Value for money
Leading	Valuing people
Original	
Open	

Add and substitute your own ideas that reflect your organisation's thinking.

TIME: Allow at least two or three hours to complete the task.

The group now discusses what seems to be really important about the organisation in which they currently work. What really matters, justifies its existence and makes it worth working for? Spend around 20 minutes doing this. It is a warming up which helps people think about values.

Hand out the Values Cards along with some Blu-Tack™. The list of values given in Box 9 are only examples. Prepare a set which is considered relevant to your organisation. For instance, a local council will not usually include profit making as a core value. Likewise a high-risk venture capital company will probably not have safety as a core value. There should be at least 20–30 cards. If you are unsure as to what values should be written on the cards make this a first exercise for you and your colleagues. Ask them to identify some core values which either are or should be what the organisation is all about.

Once you have a set of cards divide them out to the group. If there are more than five or six people divide them into smaller syndicates, giving them each a set of the Values Cards. After the Values Cards have been distributed you explain that the task is to select only five core values which the group as a whole feels most represents the vision or philosophy which should underpin the whole organisation.

These five should be put in rank order; the most important value being number one, the next most important number two and so on. To make the selection the group can stick the cards on the walls and keep rearranging them until it arrives at the final selection. Allow about 40 minutes for this work to be done.

Because there are so many values from which to choose, many of which seem important, people have to think and debate hard about which ones matter and which are less important. The task is often diffi cult and the resulting discussions and arguments can be challenging and enlightening. When the five values have been chosen the group spends up to 20 minutes discussing these, why they have emerged and what they mean.

The final task is to convert the five values into a single visionary statement reflecting the kind of organisation in which people feel they should be working.

Although this exercise may produce a vision statement it will probably not be the definitive one. It may take weeks or months to develop a truly compelling one which excites people.

In a division of the London Borough of Croydon Social Services department providing services to adults, for example, the following core values were identified:

- a planned, quality service

- responsive to users

- the independence, normality, dignity and self respect of service recipients

- improving and maintaining services

- involving users and relatives.

These were combined into a statement of the division's basic philosophy:

> We work in a planned and responsive way with the users of our service to ensure that they can live as independently as possible with dignity and self respect. The quality of our service will be improved and maintained by actively involving users and their relatives.

Similarly, Levi Strauss, the jeans and clothes maker has a vision statement which begins that it should be 'a great company' and reflect a commitment to:

> . . . excellence in everything we do and with all its constituents. We will achieve greatness through a commitment to the following goals and practices . . .

The goals and practices are then listed under headings such as: People; Customers; Retail Stores; and Suppliers.

Plenty of organisations have a vision statement, though they may not always call it that. Having articulated such a vision many organisations then breathe a sigh of relief and get on with doing what they have always done in the past. A vision only becomes a force for change when it converts inspiration into action by:

- communication – the vision is shared to gain support

- persistence – a consistency of focus, keeping moving in the right direction even when the going gets tough

- use of power – harnessing the energies and abilities of others to bring about real change

- monitoring – discovering how we are doing compared to what we want to achieve

- rearranging – altering how resources, including people, are used.

Because vision sounds mystical or metaphysical managers are sometimes reluctant to talk of 'vision' or even communicate their own view of the future in case they are thought unrealistic. The successful management of change demands that managerial leaders make others aware of the vision of the future and keep them focused on it. You have to become comfortable talking about the future in ways which command people's attention.

Though you may have doubts about how to reach the vision, there is a need to communicate hope and optimism. To sound convinced in order to be persuasive you need to be willing and able to occasionally use emotionally charged words and phrases that catch and hold people's attention. If you talk that way so will other people. Be prepared to use words which bring colour and excitement to the language. Words like success, excellence, caring, service, are not out of place. Being a good manager does not mean always appearing down to earth, highly practical and pragmatic.

In conveying their vision of both the present and the future, managerial leaders use metaphors, word pictures, imagery, parables and examples. Uncomplicated explanations or diagrams get ideas across. A company director, for instance, wanting to persuade colleagues to invest in making a new project more imaginative than originally planned explained: 'it's like the difference between black and white television and colour. Although you can do without colour, you'll much prefer it'.

As Bill Passmore, former UK Managing Director of Sun Microsystems, describes the company frequently used vivid phrases in its early presentations to convey its goal of creating an 'Open Systems' approach to the information technology industry:

> ride an industry wave rather than a single company wave . . .
> create an IT equivalent to the car industry.

Jack Welch, the famous former CEO of General Electric, summarised this need for clear and memorable expression of change goals:

> You need an overarching message, something big, but simple and understandable.

In General Electric's case, the goal was to 'revolutionise this company to have the speed and agility of a small enterprise'.

Values and business ethics

In defining the core values of the organisation, the aim is simply to distil the essence of the organisation's purpose into a form which readily communicates to a diverse workforce. In so many organisations, the value and mission statements are neutral statements of business or operational goals and style, with no wider moral or ethical implications. They may make good business sense yet they seldom touch on the truly significant or profound.

However, in recent years, there has been a growing interest in concepts such as business morality and corporate responsibility. This interest has been inspired by a variety of factors, including (in the UK at least) concerns about issues of corporate governance. It also reflects a growing awareness that organisational activity inevitably affects and is affected by the social and political society in which the organisation operates. Probably the most high profile debates in this area have centred on environmental questions such as the Exxon-Valdez incident, or the debate about the disposal of the Brent Spar platform, as well as wider discussions about environmental impact. Alongside this there have been debates about, for example, the financing of the arms industry or the effects of Third World debt.

An increasing number of organisations are beginning to argue that it is not possible to divorce the values of the organisation from the values either of the wider society or of the individuals who constitute the organisation's workforce or customers. For instance, simply in terms of employee motivation and commitment, it must be a source of concern if, as the magazine *Business Week* once reported, up to 70 per cent of managers in a number of major US corporations felt pressure to sacrifice their own personal integrity to deliver business goals. Echoing this, Peter and Waterman, in *In Search of Excellence*, commented, 'We wonder whether it is possible to be an excellent company without clarity on values and without having the right sort of values'. And even from a harder-nosed business perspective, it is becoming clear that organisations will be increasingly forced to take account of the *full* social costs of their actions, with a growing trend towards legislation on corporate responsibility.

This is not an entirely new phenomenon, and value statements such as the Johnson & Johnson 'Credo' or the 'Hewlett-Packard Way' have long included a moral dimension. However, more and more organisations are now beginning to recognise that their core values need to incorporate a diversity of interests, recognising explicitly that the organisation ultimately draws on a wide range of resources – economic, social and individual – to achieve its goals. And, in turn, if it is possible to build these diverse interests into the organisation's values this pays dividends in terms of the commitment, ownership and contribution of all parties involved.

In developing and clarifying the organisation's values, therefore, there may be benefit in not simply consulting managers or even the workforce but also in seeking the input of all the diverse parties – customers, suppliers, wider society – who may have a stake in the business or its outputs. There is growing evidence in recent research that, over the long term, the most successful organisations are those that take account of all these key interest groups. In the UK, organisations such as Body Shop or the Co-operative Bank have consciously adopted management models which build in consultation with a range of partner or interest groups, and which formally audit performance from these different perspectives. Similarly, the Centre for Tomorrow's Company initiative has drawn together a wide range of organisations, across all business sectors, to develop and promote more 'inclusive' approaches to business values. Overall, the aim is to move from a one-dimensional, financial model of business performance towards what has been described as a 'balanced business scorecard'.

In developing the organisation's value statement, therefore, there is benefit in drawing on a diversity of perspectives, to help understand the organisation's potential impact on the different groups with which it interacts. These may, for instance, include:

- shareholders

- customers

- suppliers

- society and community.

Shareholders
Shareholders typically drive the most familiar, financial business values and goals. It is clearly critical to understand their expectations and requirements from the business, but it may also be important to engage in a dialogue to ensure that they are aware of the wider context within which the organisation operates and to help move away from a short-term perspective.

Customers
Organisations are increasingly consulting their customers about their organisational goals and values (eg the Co-operative Bank's establishment of ethical investment standards based on its customers'

requirements), with the aim of building long-term customer commitment to the business.

Suppliers
More and more organisations are developing long-term strategic relationships with their suppliers, particularly as networked or outsourced arrangements become increasingly common. For many organisations, effective performance now depends on ensuring high levels of commitment all along the supply-chain, and it is likely to be critical that key suppliers understand and accept the organisation's core values.

Society and community
Organisations are now recognising that they cannot divorce themselves from the society and specific communities within which they operate (and which ultimately provide their customers and workforce). While the organisation may achieve a short-term benefit by disregarding its wider social impact, the longer-term negative effects in terms of public perception, branding, and direct legislative costs may be considerable. Although it may not be easy to consult widely, many organisations are now beginning to take account of this dimension in developing their business values and goals.

There is, of course, a danger that consulting these diverse interest groups may have a paralysing effect on the organisation, particularly if the consultation highlights some significant divergence of opinion. In practice, though, those organisations that are adopting this more inclusive, pluralist approach are finding that the ensuing debate not only throws fresh light on strategic issues but engenders a much greater commitment to the resulting values, helping the organisation to identify and address issues which might otherwise have undermined longer-term organisational performance.

Finally, be specific about your vision. Say what it would be like to visit your organisation in a few months' or years' time, once your particular vision has been realised. Describe and explain, for example, how you would be serving your customers, what kind of meetings you would be holding, what the budget would look like, how people would be spending their time and so on.

GUIDELINES

* *Build* a word picture of the preferred future

- *Define* core values and you will be close to expressing a vision of the future

- *Seek* a vision which states deeply held beliefs in the preferred future and captures people's imagination

- *Judge* vision statements by whether they excite people, not whether they are practical

- *Avoid* numbers, long words and complicated sentences in vision statements

- *In* developing and clarifying the organisation's values, seek the input of all the diverse parties – customers, suppliers, wider society – who may have a stake in the business or its outputs

- *Use* words which bring colour and excitement to the language when describing the vision

- *Talk* about the vision using metaphors, word pictures, imagery, parables, analogies, etc

- *Be* specific about your vision

- *Convert* vision to an action programme through communication, persistence, use of power, monitoring progress and rearranging how resources and people are used.

4 Commitment

Sean Taylor came from Lancashire to lead a sales team that had already seen three other managers leave. When he talked about wanting to improve the team's performance he noticed how people glanced at each other. The body language said 'What's new? We've heard all this before'.

Unlike his predecessors, Sean's move to London was a major turning point in his career. He was utterly determined to get results and worked hard to communicate this to the team by the changes he tried.

The previous managers had treated the team as separate individuals who had to reach personal sales targets. Sean intended to scrap this divisive approach. Instead he wanted a single monthly sales target for the whole team with only an average figure available for each person as a guide to what needed to be achieved.

The early reaction to his proposal was opposition. Bonuses were geared to individual sales success and the best performers were reluctant to risk financial loss. Sean adjusted his proposals while sticking to his position of wanting the change. His transparently honest belief that the change made good sense eventually convinced the team. This and other actions which he took transformed the sales figures from pedestrian to outstanding. Sean demonstrated that to make things happen you need to be concerned about:

- your personal commitment to chosen change actions, and

- the commitment of others in your organisation.

Commitment to what?

Commitment means giving all of yourself while at work. When people are committed they:

- make suggestions

- attend to detail

- welcome change

- enjoy their job

- are willing to try something new

- have pride in their work and abilities

- develop their talents and abilities

- make every minute at work useful

- get it right first time

- co-operate with others

- are trustworthy

- constantly seek improvement

- show loyalty

- make that extra effort

- acknowledge others' contributions.

Concern with building personal and workforce commitment has been growing ever since the Japanese began creating committed workforces everywhere they went.

Consultants Peter Martin and John Nicholls, who have made a special study of workforce involvement, suggest that there are three major pillars of commitment: a sense of belonging to the organisation; a sense of excitement; and confidence in management (see Figure 10).

Belonging builds the essential loyalty necessary to overcome barriers of 'them and us'. Creating a sense of excitement motivates people to perform; and confidence in management provides the right climate for commitment to flourish.

Your commitment

It is not always easy to become committed to work goals, especially if they are not entirely your own. How do you switch on the inner fire, that sense of determination that tears you from your desk, making you hungry to lead change? If you already possess that burning inner drive

Figure 10

Creating commitment

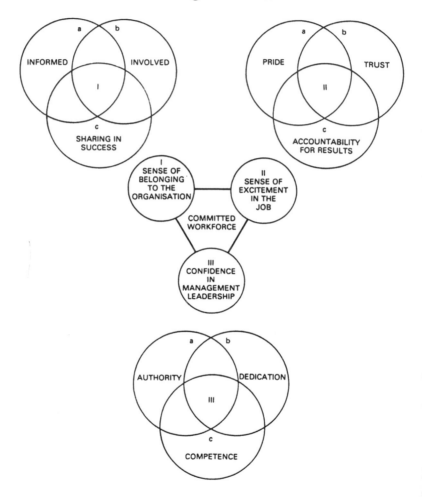

Source: *Creating a Committed Work Force*, Martin P, Nicholls J, IPM, 1987

this section of *Effective Change* will not tell you much you do not already know.

To create a commitment in others you must show that you have it yourself. Few people are convincing when riddled with doubts. A commitment to change is not merely saying you are in favour of altering the *status quo*, it is being willing to put yourself out to achieve it. The extent of your personal commitment to a particular change effort will often be decisive. People can tell when managers express commitment verbally without demonstrating it by their actions. For instance, managers who talk glibly of being committed to 'quality' must do more than create quality circles and hope that this will work. They have to be thoroughly immersed in all aspects of the issue; their personal commitment must permeate everything they touch. Similarly, technical innovation often fails because managers do not have sufficient long-term commitment, the amount required being considerable.

When you are genuinely committed to a particular course of action and openly express the strength of your feelings, without undue aggression, this can be an extremely powerful force for change. Not only do people become infected with your confidence, they will often be swayed by your sheer persistence:

A committed manager, armed with clear arguments and mobilised support, can be unstoppable.

If you find it difficult to feel the kind of commitment being described here try a version of the Chinese proverb that says you can eat anything if sliced up small enough. Find some aspect of your work or current goals, no matter how small, with which you can genuinely identify and which seems worth striving for. Keep breaking down the job or goal until you uncover some aspect relating to change that makes you feel excited, proud, interested, accountable – wanting results.

Committed managers have a thorough understanding of the final goal; they are crystal clear about what they want to achieve and can express it in simple everyday language. They can readily communicate what success (or failure) would look like; what benefits will flow from the change; what is needed to make it happen; and they are willing to fight hard for the necessary resources. They are often stubbornly unrealistic about likely obstacles, which they overcome despite the scepticism of less committed colleagues.

Persistence underpins commitment

Have you ever prised up a reluctant floorboard, or experienced the frustration of attempting to open a large packing case and finding that nothing seemed to work? Tried turning a rusty screw and wondered whether it would ever come out? Anyone with these experiences knows that not all tools work immediately. It may take persistence before what you want to achieve finally yields to your efforts. Levers of change in organisations are much the same. You cannot be sure that the particular change action you use will work instantly.

Commitment to change is a lever
which turns on the fulcrum of persistence.

Malcolm Bryant, for example, was a director of a small advertising agency which handled the recruitment advertising for a large local authority. The account was worth several hundred thousand pounds. Everything Malcolm's agency placed in the media passed through the council's central personnel department. The latter allowed Malcolm little opportunity to produce visually attractive and more effective job advertisements.

Committed to producing high quality advertisements, Malcolm regularly suggested new ways of approaching the recruitment job but the central personnel people rejected the ideas. They were happy with mere lineage, arguing that it was cheap. One day Malcolm sent a copy of his latest proposals straight to a director of one of the council's main service departments, his real customer, though strictly he should not have done so. A series of meetings followed with this particular director who insisted on running the new and more effective approach. From then on the stifling effects of the central personnel department declined, and later one of the advertisements collected an industry award for effectiveness.

The experience of successful leaders of change results are produced by underpinning commitment with dogged persistence. Refusing to retreat in the face of organisational inertia or opposition, or going for the quick fix, is crucial to leading change.

Peter Blundel, for instance, a newly appointed chief executive in a large service organisation, believed strongly that many employees possessed valuable ideas and ways of contributing to success. They were, however, often prevented from realising their potential. Promoting equal opportunities was high on his personal agenda. Shortly after his arrival a group of women employees complained to him about the behaviour of a particular senior manager. This man treated women employees in ways that Peter was determined to eradicate. 'You'll never make things different around here unless you get rid of him,' they told him.

Other staff confirmed these opinions and Peter faced pressure to sack the manager in question. He refused. Summoning the manager he asked whether he was aware of how people felt about his behaviour. The man expressed surprise, promising to reform. Six months later Peter Blundel learned that matters had not improved and he forced the man's resignation. Despite the delay Blundel's actions had considerable effect. His commitment to equal opportunities was recognised and knowledge of his persistence in acting fairly, even to those under a cloud, quickly circulated throughout the entire organisation. He had also demonstrated a consistency of focus, an ability to maintain the organisation's direction, despite pressure to act in ways which would have undermined his change effort.

Persistence also underpinned Jason Bentley's commitment as the manager of a small section in a large, decentralised organisation. His section supplied technical information. Being committed to providing an excellent service he decided that his section needed a microcomputer to develop advanced ways of handling information. Despite the need, his requests for resources received no priority.

Jason's reaction was to borrow a micro regularly from a work colleague using it to circulate new types of information. On the written material he conspicuously acknowledged the use of the loaned machine. Gradually, he was asked to produce more of the information for different people, and each time he made the point that it was being produced 'on a borrowed machine'. Finally at one meeting a senior manager asked for some data in a hurry and Jason replied cautiously that it all depended on whether he could get access to the computer. His persistence worked – he obtained his micro.

Others' commitment

'Truly involved people can do anything!' argues international management consultant Tom Peters who confesses to being 'frustrated to the point of rage' about the failure of managers to understand the need to obtain employee commitment through involvement.

Creating a commitment to change in others does not rely only on inner strength or personal powers of persuasion. There are other important ways of generating commitment and people's support for change. Involvement is merely one of the key elements in the three Pillars of Commitment described by Martin and Nicholls:

- a sense of belonging occurs when managers *inform; involve; share success*

- a sense of excitement depends on *pride; trust; accountability for results*

- confidence in leadership occurs when managers *exert authority; show dedication; display confidence.*

There are numerous ways to follow through on the above, which is really a route map for gaining commitment (see Figure 10).

Commitment plans

To obtain other people's commitment to a specific change it is sometimes worth devising a commitment plan by completing the answers to these sentences:

- The situation I specifically want to change is ....

- The people to convince whose support (or lack of opposition) is needed are ....

- To gain their commitment the detailed steps I will take are ....
  ....

- To monitor that the situation keeps moving towards the desired end state I will ....

The first of these statements encourages you to express clearly the change objectives. The second identifies people who can help and those who can throw rocks in the way. They can seldom be answered quickly. You may have to work hard to understand the feelings and motivations of other people, to gauge the best way of gaining their commitment. Sometimes you may have to compromise, accepting that the most you can achieve is that they will not block your proposals.

Agreement is not commitment. Even when people agree to changes you cannot expect everyone to be committed to them; there is a spectrum of support for change:

COMMITMENT

Total.......High.......Medium.......Low.......None

On the left of the spectrum there is you, the leader of change, who is totally or at least highly committed to a particular change effort. Other people may be anywhere to the right of you along this spectrum. The commitment plan requires that you discover where they are on this spectrum and then find ways to:

- minimise or eliminate their opposition

- move them towards your position.

Inexperienced managers who want to make things happen often mistakenly expect other people to be closer to their position than they actually are, or to be willing to move when they are not. Because some people are not close to your position or are unwilling to move does not mean that the change effort is doomed. There is always a critical mass of people whose commitment will provide the leverage for action. The number of such people who constitute a critical mass will be relatively small yet crucial to success. The exact number may be unclear since it is made up of opinion moulders. The latter are not always obvious. Decide who is needed for a critial mass of commitment and direct your plans initially at them.

Incrementalism

Incrementalism is how many successful organisations gain commitment to large shifts; it is step-by-step change which will:

• *disguise* intentions

• *create* awareness

• *develop* value changes

• *produce* facts to help convince people

• *build* consensus

• *make* dealing with complexity manageable.

Many managers like incrementalism because they realise that early decisions made before commitment and information are available can be damaging, particularly if made under stress conditions. Those with a good record of leading change do not seek major agreements in the broad, formative stage of the change process. Instead the situation is acknowledged as tentative and subject to later review.

Incrementalisim is not just muddling through. The elements of the process may be highly logical with concrete decisions being made on individual stages to gain commitment while leaving the final picture to the last possible minute.

With incrementalism managers can create pockets of commitment to their ideas. Projects are explored, options remain open and managers are opportunistic about building small, isolated commitments into a more powerful force.

This step-by-step approach may sometimes be concentrated in a very short period so that proposals are rapidly agreed and commitment fuelled by a sense of urgency and excitement.

Team-building

Team-building also generates organisation-wide commitment to a change. It focuses on goals and:

- *creates* a climate of social support for change

- *opens* up the communication process

- *gains* commitment to decisions

- *helps* achieve individual as well as organisational goals

- *builds* interdependence and team effort.

Leading change by team-building is a slow process, sometimes taking years before the full benefits are realised. It is seldom relied upon as the sole change mechanism (see also Chapter 19 on Team-Building).

GUIDELINES

- *Create* a specific commitment plan to show how you will build support for your ideas

- *Identify* groups or individuals whose support is needed

- *Develop* a strategy for gaining other people's commitment to change

- *Decide* on the critical mass of support

- *Become* unstoppable by being committed, armed with clear arguments and mobilised support

- *Show* a thorough understanding of what the final goal is all about

- *Underpin* commitment with persistence

- *Create* a sense of belonging by informing, involving and sharing success

- *Generate* excitement by developing trust, pride in and accountability for results

- *Obtain* confidence in your leadership by exerting your authority, showing dedication and displaying confidence

- *Use* incrementalism to gain support

- *Team build* to create long-term support for change.

5 Communication

A major consultancy firm recently introduced a sophisticated new electronic voicemail system for its professional staff. The potential benefits were obvious. The consultants were out of the office most of the time, and often, when in client meetings or on the road, could not be contacted directly. At the same time, effective day-to-day communication was critical to the delivery of their professional services. The new system would enable messages to be left and collected as required. Even better, it included a facility which would allow a given message to be 'copied' to multiple recipients; so, for example, a team leader could instantaneously communicate a consistent message to all members of the team.

In the event, the company's enthusiasm for the new system was short-lived. Just as, a generation earlier, the photocopier made it possible to send multiple copies of a paper document to anyone who might conceivably have an interest, so the new voicemail system soon became a conduit for communicating everything to everyone. Consultants emerged from meetings to find dozens of mostly irrelevant messages waiting. At first, they wasted time listening to them all. Then, with time always in short supply, some began to ignore the messages, and in doing so occasionally missed the single critical piece of information buried amidst the endless verbiage. In turn, staff lost confidence in the system's reliability as a communications tool, and eventually it was abandoned, to be replaced by a much simpler messaging system.

This kind of experience is familiar to us all. We live in a world where, virtually day by day, communication is becoming faster and more sophisticated. Communications media have developed more rapidly over this century than in the thousands of years that preceded, and that pace of development shows no signs of slackening. The radical developments of the past hundred years or so – the telegraph, telephone, radio, television, satellite communications – are already being enhanced or even superseded by a further range of innovations. Over the last decade, for instance, the business environment has seen an explosion of new communications media – facsimile, voicemail, electronic mail, teleconferencing, the Internet and numerous others.

Yet, as the consultants' experience shows, more communication does not necessarily mean better. For many of us the problem now is not too little information but too much. We switch on our PCs in the morning to find numerous e-mails waiting for us, most of them trivial or unimportant. In our supposedly 'paperless' offices, we find ourselves buried under mounds of unnecessary photocopies. We search for data on the World Wide Web, only to find ten thousand options facing us. In the end we are none the wiser and considerably less well informed. The question, then, is how to make communications work for us.

In the context of change this question becomes critical. Effective communications are a critical element in the successful management of change. In previous chapters we discussed the importance of leadership, of vision and values, and of commitment. All of these factors, each in itself key to delivering successful organisational change, are worthless if they cannot be communicated. Some of this communication will no doubt be personal and face-to-face. However, particularly in large organisations, this direct contact will generally need to be reinforced by a range of other, more diverse channels – written communications, presentations, briefings, electronic media, and so on.

At a more basic level, too, we need to communicate the rationale and detail of the proposed change. Why is change necessary? Why are these particular steps being taken? What practical impact will the changes have? What kind of actions or response will be needed from employees? These are all simple questions, but many change programmes have foundered because the answers have not been effectively communicated to the staff. In too many organisations, change is just something that happens to the workforce, often in a series of apparently contradictory shockwaves, with no one taking the time or trouble to explain what is going on or why (what one commentator called the BOHICA syndrome – Bend Over, Here It Comes Again).

Communicating change

Effective communication, therefore, is key to any successful change initiative. We need to communicate, clearly and consistently, what is going on and why. We must ensure that there is full understanding of the rationale for change, and its aims, and of the various activities or steps that will contribute to the overall process. This means ensuring that all those involved fully grasp the vision, commitment and values of the change-leaders. And, on a continuing basis, it implies that all relevant information about the change process is appropriately and efficiently channelled around the organisation.

This may be difficult to achieve in practice. Organisational change is generally a problematic and stressful process for all involved. Effective communication is often undermined by precisely those factors that make communications so critical. On the one hand, the anxiety and uncertainty that inevitably accompanies change usually means that the rumour mill is working overtime, with the worst interpretation being placed on even the most innocuous development. On the other, under the strain of a fast-moving or demanding change process, standard communication channels may fail because people see them as inappropriate or low priority. We become too busy to hold our regular management meeting, or to publish our periodic newsletter, and in any case things are moving too quickly for that. The result is that we allow the grapevine to take over and, not surprisingly, find that anxieties increase and commitment to the change process is undermined.

Developing a communication strategy

If we are to avoid these pitfalls, we need to ensure that, right from the start, effective communication is built into the fabric of the change process. This means, in effect, that we need to establish a communication strategy that runs parallel to our plans for change, with appropriate communication activities to underpin each element and stage of the change process.

The range and mix of the communications processes to be used will depend on the nature and scope of the change process itself. Different communication channels are appropriate to different types of communication, and it is likely that communication needs will vary as the change process progresses. Our communication requirements during initial planning, for example, may well be very different from our requirements when we are dealing with the practical implementation of particular changes. At each stage in the process, we need to ensure that we have the right mix of communication activity, providing the right information at the right time to the right people.

Expressed in these terms this objective appears rather daunting. After all, change is hard enough without also having to worry about who we are going to communicate with! In practice, though, with some careful preliminary thought, it is often possible to develop a very simple but highly-focused approach to communication which will significantly improve the overall effectiveness of the change process. In many cases, too, the result is less, rather than more, communication – information targeted where it is required, rather than scattered indiscriminately. In the modern organisation – as with our consultants at the start of the chapter – the problem is often too much data, rather than not enough.

Planning communications

In planning the communication strategy, we need first of all to identify the key stages in the change process. These might typically include:

- initial assessment of the need for change

- development and evaluation of potential change options

- detailed planning of the selected option

- implementation of planned changes

- review of the overall process and its outcomes.

In practice, particularly in relatively small-scale change, these various stages may become telescoped. Nevertheless, the communication needs at each stage may be very different, and particular types or levels of communication may be appropriate (and, perhaps even more important, *inappropriate*) at each point.

In the past, managers sometimes talked guardedly about 'the need to know', which often became a euphemism for non-communication ('We're not telling the staff because they don't need to know . . .'). And yet, approached with an open mind, the principle remains a good one. At each stage in the process, the starting point is to ask: Who has a need to know about this, and what information do they need? If we focus on this group and its needs, our communication is likely to be more effective than if we adopt a 'scatter-gun' approach across the organisation.

If we apply this principle to the stages outlined above, we may find that, for instance, during the initial assessment and development phases, the communication needs are quite limited. We may be communicating largely at senior management levels, perhaps within the area under review or perhaps with key stakeholders or customers. We may need to ensure that relevant senior managers understand the drivers for change, and the potential implications of whatever steps we take. Equally, we will wish to consult with those who are likely to be affected by whatever steps we might take. To support this process, we might need to communicate detailed data about costs and benefits, perhaps presenting a number of scenarios to enable choices to be made.

During this phase, therefore, the scope of our communication is likely to be relatively narrow, but we may well be presenting or gathering some highly detailed data to inform our decisions. Our channels of communication will be relatively formal – detailed reports or presentations, extended and structured interviews or discussions. Much of the communication will be one-to-one, or in small groups. The focus will generally be on hard, objective, impersonal data rather than on personal vision or commitment (although, of course, the latter qualities may well be needed to overcome the opposition or challenges encountered during these stages).

More controversially, applying the 'need to know' principle, we might also explicitly decide to *exclude* certain groups from the communication process at this stage. Most commonly, organisations may decide that there should be no communication with the wider workforce until definite decisions have been made. When a well-known service company was recently contemplating rationalising a number of its administrative centres, the feasibility of the proposal was initially considered by a small senior management team behind closed doors. Various options were explored, their respective implications examined, and then the selected proposal was announced. From this point onwards, communication and consultation was expanded to a much wider constituency (including the workforce and trade unions), as the detailed implementation plans were developed. In handling the communication in this way, management had judged that, until a clear decision had been made, communication about the review would have simply stirred up anxieties without offering any meaningful benefit to the workforce.

Although openness is often the best policy, it is impossible to be prescriptive about how this kind of communication should be handled. It depends on factors such as:

- *the nature of the change being contemplated*
  How definite is it?
  How threatening are its implications?
  Who will be affected?

- *the extent to which employees might contribute to the decision process*
  Does the workforce have detailed knowledge not easily available to the senior team?

- *the culture of the organisation*
  Is openness seen as paramount?
  Are people comfortable living with a degree of uncertainty?

By contrast with the above example, when Royal Mail undertook a major reorganisation of its national structure a few years ago; there was full communication with all those affected from the earliest opportunity. In this case, the judgement was that the uncertainty involved was more than outweighed by the potential contribution that staff could make to developing and implementing the new structure.

Overall, therefore, in planning the communication strategy, we need to ask:

- What are the key phases of the change process?

- At each phase, which groups do we need to communicate with? And, conversely, do we wish to maintain any kind of confidentiality?

- What is the nature, scope and level of information that needs to be communicated to each group?

- What are the most appropriate mechanisms for communicating the required data simply and effectively at each stage and to each group?

The last point here is particularly important. Even when serious consideration is given to communication planning, there is often a temptation to apply a single solution ('We'll produce a monthly newsletter to let everyone know what's going on'). In practice, no one approach is likely to meet the varying communication requirements that will arise during the course of a significant change process – if, for instance, we produce a newsletter that incorporates all the detail required by the various participants, it is likely that many will be simply overwhelmed by the quantity of data provided.

Furthermore, it is likely that the purpose of our communication will vary between different constituencies and at different stages in the process – we may wish to inform decision-making, to provide factual operational data, to inspire or enthuse, to seek feedback, or simply to ensure common understanding. All of these are legitimate elements of a communications strategy, but each will require a significantly different approach. How, then, do we evaluate our needs and identify the most appropriate mechanisms?

Analysing communication needs

Once we have identified the target-groups for communication at each stage, we then need to consider what kind of communication is required. And, again, we need to start with a basic question: what is the purpose of the communication?

Although this seems an obvious starting-point, it is a question which is frequently overlooked in practice. We tend to assume that communication is, in itself, a good thing, and we therefore rush to kick off the process, without really thinking through our goals and so end up with inappropriate form or content. In reality, different communication goals are likely to involve different types of information. These might, for instance, include:

- strategic information (eg about long-term goals or objectives)

- speculative or hypothetical information (eg scenarios or implications arising from potential decisions)

- cost/benefit information

- operational information (eg specific process or regulatory requirements arising from changes)

- cultural or attitudinal information (eg relating to the style or values associated with current or proposed change).

Although any given communication may involve a mix of some (or, indeed, all) of the above, the proportions will vary enormously, depending on the purpose of the communication. A senior management communication intended to inform decision-making or decision-ratification might focus on strategic information (why are we making these

Box 10

Information	Audience	Most Appropriate Media
Strategic	Senior management	Formal report or presentation
	General workforce	Newsletter or presentation
Speculative or hypothetical	Senior management	Formal report or consultative presentation
	General workforce	Presentation with extended opportunity for discussion or questions
Cost/benefit	Senior management	Formal report or presentation, graphics
	General workforce	Formal newsletter or presentations, mainly graphics
Operational information	Senior management	Formal paper or memo
	General workforce	Newsletter, notice or memo
Cultural information	Senior management	Face-to-face presentation or discussion
	General workforce	Direct presentation, video, 'informal' newsletters

changes?) supported by detailed hypothetical and cost/benefit data. By contrast, a general staff communication intended to promote commitment to a change might well use cultural or attitudinal data to underpin some relatively simple strategic information. The first communication is likely to be comparatively factual and objective, whereas the second might be more subjective, perhaps 'selling' a personal vision of the proposed changes. And, by extension, it may be appropriate to use different media to communicate – the first might be a written paper or report, whereas the second is perhaps more effectively communicated through a presentation or video.

At each stage in the change process, then, we will need to communicate a different mix of information to different audiences, and the combination of these factors will generally determine the most appropriate communications medium. In practice, the influencing factors will often be complex (and will also include elements such as the overall culture of the organisation and the skills and characteristics of the individuals involved), so it is impossible to be prescriptive about the most appropriate medium in each case. Nevertheless, in general, particular types of media tend to be more appropriate to particular audiences and types of information. In Box 10, for example, we illustrate the kinds of media that might be appropriate to communicate the above types of data to, respectively, a senior management or a more general audience.

Although most communications will incorporate a range of information types, we should identify our priorities for each communication and select the media accordingly. We should also aim not to be overly ambitious – it is tempting, under the stress of a change process, to try to bundle all our communication needs into a single vehicle at each stage. So, for example, we find newsletters or briefings which include, say, an inspirational piece by the CEO, an outline of progress in working towards the change objectives, some quantitative data on performance, and perhaps some operational guidelines about new processes, all in the space of a few pages. At best, half of this will be left unread – readers skim through the CEO's piece and fail to notice a piece of critical operational information on the back page. At worst, the various messages may seem contradictory or confusing – the CEO's words of inspiration perhaps undermined by apparently poor performance figures or by implied criticism of operational practices.

If possible, it is preferable to focus on the essence of each communication goal and keep the lines of communication separate. Where different types of data are provided, these should be mutually reinforcing and clearly linked. The CEO's inspirational message, for instance, might well be linked to encouraging performance data or to detailing operational changes designed to support business goals – but, if so, these links should be clearly spelled out. If we simply have two different sets of information to communicate, it is better that these are kept separate. We might, for instance, use a staff newspaper or a video to communicate the CEO's message, but then use another briefing channel to communicate performance data.

Two-way communication

So far in this chapter, we have primarily discussed 'top down' communication – that is, from senior management to the workforce. In practice, the effective management of change – probably more than any other facet of organisational life – also requires high quality 'bottom up' communication. As we see elsewhere in this book, there are countless potential barriers to change – personal, psychological, structural, operational and so on. If we are to overcome these, it is important that we have a clear understanding of what people are thinking. Are the change proposals and imperatives well understood? Are they accepted? What kinds of barriers or problems do people perceive at the front line? How well are things working in practice? What could be done better?

Our communications strategy, therefore, also needs to enable people to provide appropriate upwards feedback. During the course of a change process, we may wish to use a variety of media which provide opportunities for different levels and types of feedback. These might, for instance, include:

- open briefing sessions with opportunities for discussion or questions

- formal employee surveys to allow staff to provide anonymous feedback

- focus group sessions to enable more wide-ranging discussion of particular issues

- consultation with trade unions, staff councils or other representative bodies

- use of electronic mail or similar channels to encourage feedback

- quality circles or review teams to address particular aspects of the change process.

In addition to eliciting feedback, many of these channels also provide opportunities to develop mutually acceptable ways of dealing with controversial aspects of the change proposals. For example, an increasing number of organisations are now developing 'partnership' relationships with trade unions, enabling the two sides to work jointly to develop constructive ways of handling change. Although the dialogue may be problematic, the intention is that the resulting outcome is fully 'owned' by both parties, rather than simply being imposed and grudgingly tolerated. Although most of these partnership arrangements are still in their infancy, the basic principles will be recognised by most managers. If we want to 'sell' a controversial proposal, we are more likely to achieve genuine buy-in by engaging in serious debate at the start than by simply imposing our authority.

Piecing together the strategy

Overall, therefore, the communications strategy needs to provide appropriate reinforcement to the change process by communicating, at each stage, the right information to the right audience through the most suitable media. Expressed in these terms the task sounds daunting – in practice, though, the key objective is often simplicity. We are not necessarily aiming to communicate more – we are aiming to communicate better.

In many cases, indeed, effective communication will involve simplifying or reducing what is already there. It is no accident, for example, that organisations such as Proctor and Gamble insist that memos should be limited to one page, and reports to no more than four or five pages. As we begin to piece together the elements of the communications strategy, we should be asking ourselves at each stage: what is the core message we wish to communicate? We should then focus ruthlessly on that message, not through over-simplification, but by aiming to eliminate the 'white noise' that tends to surround most organisational discourse.

Planned on this basis, the overall communications strategy will probably incorporate a range of complementary communications activities, with the precise mix varying across the life of the project. For example, in one major public sector organisation, restructuring the communications process included:

- *periodic briefing papers to the board produced by the change project team and its subgroups.* These were produced to a standard format, and provided factual information in a concise format. They served a range of communication purposes, but in each case the purpose (and the resulting response required from the Board) was clearly specified – categories included, for instance, 'for action', 'for decision/ratification' or 'for information only'.

- *briefing newsletters for all affected staff.* These were produced in a short, accessible, 'tabloid' format, and were designed to convey factual and operational information about the restructurings. They included some standard features so that staff could track progress. The newsletter was produced at least every few months but during the most intense periods of change more frequent copies were published.

- *occasional briefings from the chief executive designed to convey senior management commitment to the process, particularly during more problematic phases.* This was supplemented at one key point in the project by a corporate video.

- *at critical stages in the project management conferences, which formed the basis of cascaded team briefs.* The aim of these was not simply to provide 'top down' information but also to provide a forum for upwards feedback and discussion on the project. In support of this, the organisation also ran a formal employee survey following completion of the first phase of implementing the changes. Alongside this, the organisation also maintained continuing discussions (including, where appropriate, formal negotiations) with its recognised trade unions.

Across the two-year life of the change project, these communications activities actually constituted a relatively small investment of time and effort (and, indeed, in terms of overall volume of activity, was probably little more than standard practice in the organisation). However, the careful targeting of the various elements ensured that all parties received the information they needed in a timely and efficient manner, and that all key messages were communicated clearly and precisely. At the same time, staff generally felt that their voices had been listened to in the planning and implementation of the changes.

Although this is a relatively sophisticated example relating to a large-scale change exercise, the same principles apply regardless of the size or scale of the changes involved. If we are managing even a small-scale restructuring in a single team or department, we should still identify the communications needs or goals at each stage and select the most appropriate communications media to deliver these. In a small group, we will probably conduct much of the communication face-to-face, through interviews, discussions and presentations. However, at specific points other media may be more appropriate – for example, a written note or memo to ensure consistent understanding of new operational processes, or the involvement of a third-party to collect objective feedback on the changes.

GUIDELINES

- *Communicate*, clearly and consistently, what is going on and why. Ensure that there is full understanding of the rationale for change, of the aims of the change programme, and of the various activities or steps that will contribute to the overall process

- *Ensure* that, right from the start, effective communication is built into the fabric of the change process

- *At each stage* in the process, ensure the right mix of communication activity, providing the right information at the right time to the right people

- *Decide* who to include (and, if appropriate, who to exclude) from the communication process at each stage

- *At each stage* in the change process, select the mix of information appropriate to each audience, and choose communications media accordingly

- *Establish* channels to allow appropriate upwards feedback, using a variety of media to provide opportunities for different levels and types of response

- *Focus* on the key messages, not through over-simplification, but by aiming to eliminate 'white noise'.

6 Power and influence

Long before Machiavelli started his management consultancy to princes in distress, power was a dirty word. Managers seldom discuss it openly. Those who do are usually people who feel powerless, rather than those who already have it.

Politics and power are loaded words: those who understand the former and possess the latter seldom use the terms. We have become expert instead of avoiding the words 'managerial power' by using another language:

- let managers manage

- he's very influential

- he's got real clout

- carries weight with the chairman

- she's tough minded

- she's obstructive

- he can be difficult

- has the Director's ear

- you'll need to persuade . . .

- you keep hearing her name mentioned

- she is very persuasive

- there's a lot of politics here

- she is very controlling

- he has access to a lot of resources

- everybody goes to her for advice.

In fact talking about your management power may well produce embarrassment or a response as if you are revealing your sex life. What then is power? At its simplest it is the ability to induce or influence behaviour. As no single explanation seems to satisfy everyone, the following meaning is used here:

Power is a measure of your potential to:
get others to do what you want them to do or
avoid being forced by others to do what you don't want to do.

Power is what you give other people. That is to say, people acquire authority to get others to do what they want them to do mainly because those people are *willing* to let them exercise power. An example of this is when a new manager joins an organisation; in the early days people may be unwilling to argue with or oppose this new person whose power to make things happen is not yet known. Thus, in the first six months the new manager may be able to exercise more influence in making significant changes that at a later stage when he is well established.

The most effective managers are not always those who are the most pleasant or have the strongest need to achieve change. Research shows that the most effective managers are the ones who have a high need for power, are highly self controlled and who channel their power in socially desirable directions. This means involving subordinates in shared or collaborative approaches rather than appearing to dominate and control everything.

Nor is power a fixed quantity, although there may be a limit to how much one person can acquire. Managerial power can be likened to a plant that needs cultivating – depending on what fertiliser you use and how it is applied the faster the growth can be.

Major organisational change is in one sense revolutionary. It is overturning the *status quo*, creating a new reality with new relationships, roles and objectives. Power is certainly a crucial component, as some major changes can only be achieved through using power and authority to compel compliance. Neither power nor formal planning systems, however, fully explain how strategic change occurs.

Since power is certainly essential for achieving major change most managers want it, even if they seldom admit to the fact. As a first step in trying to expand your power you need to ask 'How much power do I have at present?'

Checking out your power

To check out your power consider your present situation. For instance, how sensitive are you to where power exists in your organisation? It is easy to point to a senior manager and say that he or she has a lot of power. The reality is that less senior people can also acquire considerable power without being in a high status role.

Margaret Allen was a personnel officer in a local government department, seconded there from the central personnel service. Officially she reported to the head of the personnel service, but in practice she was so embedded in the department to which she had been seconded that she had almost a free hand. She gained the trust of the department and gradually managers at all levels came to ask for her advice. They even joked about going to see 'Aunty Marge'. By the time she retired Margaret had acquired power in the department far beyond her formal job description.

Thus, in reviewing your own power position, do not assume that being in a junior position is necessarily a reason for preventing you from gaining power and influence.

Managers who do succeed at gaining power are usually extremely sensitive to where power exists in their organisation. They are alert to who has influence on whom and how. In considering your own power position, review who, in your organisation, seems to make things happen, regardless of their position in the formal structure. Identifying who has the power takes you halfway to discovering how to turn it to your own account.

Increasing your own power is like any other kind of investment. You may have to take calculated risks with your initial supply, investing it in activities and decisions which will produce a return in terms of added power. For example, Maurice Jones was a middle manager in a company that needed to improve its record on equal opportunities. Top management created a committee to make proposals and to see through the necessary changes.

Other managers saw the subject as uncongenial because no one really knew how much commitment to improving equal opportunities was really being made by the top management. Despite these risks, Maurice Jones offered to chair the new committee and once appointed set about organising an in-house survey. On behalf of the committee he presented the results to top management. Though the survey findings were not particularly congenial, the presentation raised Maurice's personal profile in the organisation and whenever issues to do with equal opportunity were being discussed he tended to be invited to attend.

When the committee reported its proposals for change Maurice again played a prominent role and was asked to lead the next phase of implementation. This covered a wide variety of the company's areas of operation; there were soon several project groups created and Maurice was asked to help steer their activities. Within a year Maurice had acquired considerable power and influence, gaining the ear of several top managers and improving his own personal chances of promotion.

Has your career path moved you towards key sources of power in the organisation? When thinking about your next career move give some thought to whether it takes you closer to where the power lies, as well as whether it is better paid or more interesting. Anyone posted abroad from a large company soon comes to realise their increased isolation and vulnerability. The lines of communication with those in power are extended and perhaps weakened. More than one manager has done extremely well in a foreign posting only to return home to find that they have been away too long from those in real power and that their future prospects are now worse, not better.

Do you use your power to influence and manage people upon whom you are dependent? There is little point in gaining power if you do not exercise it to get things done. People need to see your power in action to help them do their jobs better. Successfully using your power and influence to achieve an objective has a multiplier effect. Power used well leads to gaining more power.

Do people see you as powerful and influential? One way of gaining increased power and influence is to convince others that you already have a considerable amount. Putting this across is what leadership is about and why personality is so crucial.

Finally, do you really recognise that all your actions can affect your power? Like Maurice Jones, mentioned above, managers with power tend to have a high visibility in the organisation. The greater your visibility the more likely that anything you do will directly or indirectly affect your power. What meetings you attend, who you have lunch with, who you ask for help can all have an impact.

By the same token, it is important to avoid any actions which could accidentally decrease your power and influence. Powerful managers tend to pick objectives carefully and make sure they are both desirable and attainable. They avoid fighting battles they cannot win.

Suppose, for example, that you are a manager charged with introducing a computerised personnel information system. You will quickly discover that one option for creating the new system is linking with the organisation's payroll package. Such a move, though, may meet stiff resistance from the financial experts, concerned to protect their system from contamination. In this situation, a predictable way to lose power is to insist that the new personnel system cannot happen without being linked with the payroll. Such an insistence may eventually kill the project which will also affect your power and influence. Even if you win the argument it may permanently damage your relationships with powerful connections elsewhere in the organisation.

Types of power
Managers possess several kinds of power, using them at different times in varying quantities. You can get things done and achieve change through:

- *coercive power* – making things happen by fear, threats or punishment

- *expertise* – others comply because of your knowledge or skills

- *role position* – use of authority from your job or location in the organisation; includes control of important resources

- *rewards* – ability to reward emotionally and financially; includes the persuasive skills associated with leadership and personality

- *connections* – access to networks, membership of groups in and out of the organisation and hence social power. Establishing favourable relationships is based on:

  creating a sense of obligation
  developing a strong professional reputation
  identification of others with the manager
  perceived dependence.

In thinking about your own power it is thus worth reviewing:

On what is my present power based?

Dependency

In understanding power and then using it for achieving change, every manager should be aware of dependency.

The more power you acquire the more likely you will become dependent on other people. As the above definition of power suggests, an ability to get others to do things also means being dependent on their efforts. This experience of increasing dependency on others can be puzzling and indeed frustrating, particularly for newer managers who have perhaps trained in a narrow professional area and are now gaining wider responsiblities.

Instead of promotion ensuring that you can get more things done and quicker, you may find that the reverse is true. Because you no longer do everything yourself, changes take even longer to produce than before. The extent of management dependency is often not recognised. You may, for example, be dependent on:

- your boss

- your boss's boss

- your peer group

- unions

- subordinates

- subordinates of subordinates

- customers

- suppliers

- competitors

- statutory bodies

- community organisations.

The need for power is thus more to do with handling dependency than being power hungry or the urge to get ahead. Your job demands that you plan, organise, budget and control, yet it does not automatically supply the right amount of authority to achieve these ends. Your dependency on other people is always greater than the power and control inherent in your job or position.

The number of people on whom a manager is dependent and over whom no direct authority is exercised, has steadily risen. In one Japanese bank, for example, in defiance of neat theories about span of control, one manager has several hundred branch managers reporting directly to him. Similarly, the number of people who can affect a manager's performance has tended to increase. The first basic lesson emerging from the reality of dependency is:

Identify those on whom you are most dependent.

This means being willing to acknowledge your dependency, not acting as if you are the only source of authority to get things done. Indeed one of the quickest ways to lose power and influence is to act as if you are always the prime mover, the principal source of ideas, or the only person who really gets results. The second lesson from the reality of dependency is:

**Broaden your support so that when you need help
it can be obtained from multiple sources.**

Networking is the ability to create an interlinked group of people who have things in common and who assist one another in getting things done. These may be contacts, personal connections and other linkages on which you can call. You can widen your support in various other ways, including creating obligations. This may involve looking for opportunities to do favours for certain people, helping them when they have a problem, being willing to share knowledge and information and so on.

Research into how power is actually used by successful managers also provides some practical suggestions for action.

First, managers controlling resources valued by others or seen as being important tend to use a greater variety of influence strategies than those with less power. The practical lessons from this are:

**Examine closely whether you are relying too much on
one strategy for achieving change.**

**Explore ways to widen the variety of influence strategies
and tactics used in exercising power.**

How could you go about developing a more varied approach to using influence? You will tend to use one of the following tactics to make things happen:

- reason

- friendliness

- creating coalitions

- bargaining

- assertiveness

- relying on higher authority

- sanctions.

While using a mixture of tactics, successful change makers do not attempt to use them all. They tend to rely heavily on skills and knowledge combined with reason to make things happen. Less experienced managers try using all seven approaches to gain influence, but as a result they usually complete fewer objectives and are probably using these tactics indiscriminately.

Secondly, managers with power use assertiveness more frequently than those with less power. Assertiveness is based more on personality and leadership skills than possession of organisational power. The lessons for practical action are:

Gaining power means being willing to be assertive, and being assertive will often attract power.

See also Assertiveness in Chapter 20 on Verbal Skills.

Widening your influence

Since power and influence are hard to measure, increasing them may seem purely a matter of management flair and leadership skills. But it is possible to be rather more systematic in analysing the factors that lead to increased influence.

You can conduct a circles of influence exercise either on your own or with your management team. When done properly it takes about an hour and teases out new ways of tackling what sometimes are apparently insoluble problems.

On a large sheet of paper or a flipchart draw three circles as shown in Figure 11. Circle A contains problems that either you or your team can solve completely with no outside assistance. Circle B contains problems over which either you or your team have influence without complete control. Finally, Circle C contains problems or forces affecting you or the team that are completely outside your influence.

A circle of influence analysis can be carried out by following the steps shown in Box 11. The final step can produce surprising revelations, challenging the negative idea that you or the team are powerless over a particular situation. Instead, you begin inventing ways of taking back power and acquiring influence where before you felt that you had little or none.

Figure 11

Circles of influence diagram

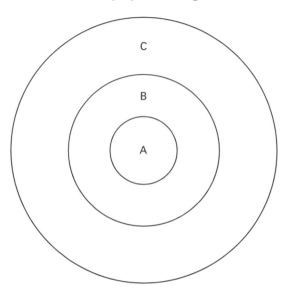

Box 11

Circles of influence exercise

Step 1   Spend 10 minutes listing the problems currently causing concern. If you do this with your team, each member writes down
their own particular list.

Step 2   Once the problem list is completed it is written on a flipchart. If
there are several lists these are combined to eliminate duplica-
tions. Each problem is clarified to avoid vagueness.

Step 3   Review each problem to decide in which circle of influence it
falls. If a team does the exercise there has to be consensus on
each problem as to where it falls in the circles. The problem is
recorded on the diagram by a brief title or code letter.

Step 4   The final stage is the creative one. You, or the team, try to think
of ways of extending the boundaries of circles A and B to
increase your influence over the forces that are affecting the situation. You ask: 'How could we move an item from further out to
further in?'

GUIDELINES

- *Identify* your own power skills

- *Analyse* whether your career path is moving you towards key sources of power in the organisation

- *Use* your power to influence and manage those on whom you are dependent

- *Assess* whether others see you as powerful and influential and if not why not

- *Assume* that all your actions can affect your power; avoid actions which can accidentally decrease it

- *Recognise* that the greater your power the more you will be dependent on others

- *Seek* power to handle dependency

- *Identify* those on whom you are most dependent

- *Broaden* your support so that when you need help it can be obtained from multiple sources

- *Examine* whether you are over-reliant on one strategy of influence for achieving change

- *Use* assertiveness to gain power

- *Conduct* a Circles of Influence exercise to analyse how to extend influence

- *Check* who has the power and is dependent on whom

- *Seek* ways to gain control over tangible resources, such as budgets, people, buildings and equipment

- *Find* ways to control useful information and information channels

- *Spend* time developing relationships and gathering information; take low cost, high pay-off actions first.

7 Resistance to change

Rupert Murdoch acquired *The Times* and *The Sunday Times* from the Thomson Organisation. On meeting Harold Evans, *The Sunday Times'* editor, he told him: 'I'm going to make a clean sweep of management. I'm fixing the redundancies tomorrow.'

Murdoch used a blunt instrument because he had no faith in the existing management team and wanted anyone who could resist the changes out of the way. Some years later, when introducing major technological change into his newspapers, he sacked the entire printing staff, which led to the famous Wapping siege. Once again, he was ruthless in dealing with resistance.

Resistance is so common that it is a part of the change process which all managers need to know about and have ideas on how to deal with. Resistance is:

Any conduct that tries to maintain the *status quo* in the face of pressure to change it.

The *status quo* is thus the pivot on which resistance revolves. When trade unions, for example, are mistrustful of proposals their concern is usually with the extent to which the *status quo* will alter, who will be affected and how.

When one thinks of trade unions, one usually thinks of resistance as a form of active opposition, perhaps involving go-slows, walkouts and strikes. The word *sabotage* in fact comes from the word *sabot* or shoe. At the start of the industrial revolution French workers were known to throw their *sabots* – shoes – into the machine to destroy the mechanisation of their workplaces. Yet, equally, resistance can be passive, showing itself when employees are demoralised, demotivated and unwilling to co-operate in a constructive way to support change.

When managers seek change they are seldom merely tinkering with tangibles like machinery. They are also directly or indirectly affecting the ongoing processes within the organisation. These processes may well involve relationships such as who reports to whom, who has contact with whom, and so on. Interfering with such relationships may generate conflict and hence resistance.

Types

When trying to make things happen you are likely to meet various kinds of resistance such as:

- cultural

- social

- organisational

- psychological.

Cultural resistance occurs when the values which are built into the organisation are affected. People live by these values, and in some organisations it may be important to preserve face. Changes which do not allow this may generate both conflict and resistance. The organisation may have certain traditions which for years people have accepted and in some cases planned their life around. An example of this is where it has become custom and practice for someone to be sent on specialised training after being in a particular job for several years. On their return the expectation may be that they will then gain further promotion. If management decides that this tradition is no longer efficient or justified there may be considerable repercussions in trying to alter it.

Social resistance happens when changes threaten to affect relationships. For instance, the changes may appear to damage group solidarity or teamwork which people want to protect. Or perhaps the changes challenge conformity to existing norms. It may, for example, be accepted tradition that the organisation does not impinge on people's holidays and weekends. A manager who decides to hold training sessions at the weekend may meet considerable opposition.

Organisational resistance takes place when the changes seem likely to interfere with formal arrangements which people have come to accept as the *status quo*; for example, when the changes seem to affect status differentials, or impact on who is where in the hierarchy. It may also arise when the changes seem likely to alter or threaten certain people's power and influence.

Pscyhological resistance involves selective perception. Change is seen as detrimental, not beneficial, which leads to conservatism and conformity.

While you may not always know which type of resistance you are meeting, and the above classification does not really explain why it occurs, knowing about the different types of resistance can be a useful tool for starting to analyse the issues.

Another useful way of analysing resistance is to consider its:

- intensity

- source

- focus.

Try to judge the intensity of resistance, since this may offer a guide as to how you should respond, and indeed whether you may hope to overcome it and how long that might take.

The source of resistance is sometimes hard to judge. There are often many hidden agendas. People are influenced by values, facts and beliefs so that uncovering the source may be helpful in developing a strategy for suitable action.

The focus or location of the resistance could be within you, in other people or in the work environment.

There are as many reasons why resistance arises as there are managers. Broadly though the reasons can be reduced to:

Behavioural factors such as emotional reasons

Rational or system factors.

Each situation generates its own set of circumstances. Box 12 identifies some of the better-known general causes. Resistance to technological innovation has also been the subject of considerable research in recent years and some of the causes are shown in Box 13. The commonest reason for resisting technological change is perhaps management's psychological and emotional mindset. This stems from a reluctance to make mistakes, a belief that a new idea or product must be as successful or profitable as the current winner on which the firm has grown.

Coming to terms with resistance

Understandably many managers consider resistance to their proposals with distaste; opposition is seen as a negative force creating unwelcome obstacles. This interpretation of resistance is increasingly being questioned.

Box 12

Why people resist change in organisations

- A desire not to lose something of value – insecurity; advancement
- Historical factors – how previous changes have been handled
- How the change is being handled
- Misunderstanding of the change and its implications – lack of information; no perceived benefits
- Belief that the change does not make sense for the organisation
- Uncertainty about how much freedom there is to do things differently
- Lack of decision-making skills
- Inexperience of implementing change; reluctance to experiment
- Existing psychological and social commitments to current products, processes and organisations; strong peer group norms
- Complacency
- Powerful trade union attitudes to change methods
- Complexity – frustration caused by technical problems; fear of uncertainty
- Management wants change – therefore resist it!

Box 13

Reasons for resistance to technological change

- Psychological and social commitments to existing products, processes and the organisational arrangements
- Large capital investments in long life, single use facilities
- Low initial profits and reduced rate of growth
- Small-size or fragmented activites
- Complacent top management
- Industrial norms; associations or cartels which perpetuate industry bound thinking
- Lack of successful entrepreneurial models to copy
- Labour opposition to change methods
- Complexity
- Management failing to listen and respond to issues such as job security

First, there are those who would advocate abandoning altogether the concept of resistance. Being such an all-embracing term it hardly helps matters except to provide a rather fuzzy label for a set of complex behaviours. It fails to reveal, for instance, why on some days people may be enthusiastic for change yet resist it on other days; and it makes no allowance for the fact that today's resisters may be tomorrow's supporters.

Secondly, some people, particularly psychologists who have studied the problem of resistance in some depth, have argued that resistance to organisational change is perfectly rational rather than merely irrational. Why people resist change suggests that, from their standpoint, resistance may be exactly the right thing correctly based on self interest. It may even be in the interest of the organisation itself.

So resistance can be seen as a positive asset. By challenging assumptions it helps stimulate the development of mutually acceptable goals. Instead of managers simply announcing the end result they intend to achieve, resistance may modify it and in the process make it more realistic and acceptable.

Resistance to change can also help to prevent stagnation. For instance, when a trade union challenges certain management changes it may throw light on far more fundamental issues that need addressing, such as the effects on the quality of the product or the service being provided by the organisation. In opposing shipyard closures, for example, unions have often sought to draw management's attention to new or neglected market opportunities or new ways to reduce costs.

Resistance also stimulates curiosity, allowing problems to be aired and alternative solutions to be discussed. It can be a necessary cost of personal and social change. Thus a balanced view of resistance reveals that it is not always counter-productive nor to be opposed at all costs. It is part of the normal checks and balances within an organisation, and in many cases can be considered a healthy element protecting the *status quo*.

A good example of this happening occurred when a manager in a local authority wanted to alter the arrangements in a number of buildings staffed by a mixture of manual and salaried staff. The new arrangements offered the opportunity for many of the manual workers to become salaried staff and from the management's viewpoint offered the chance to recruit higher calibre staff who would work more flexibly. There was considerable resistance from the trade unions to the proposals. Discussions revealed that the unions in fact liked the proposals. What they objected to was an arrangement in which certain long-standing employees would have their existing jobs deleted and be asked to apply for the new jobs. Once the management agreed to allow people to choose for themselves, either to apply for the new jobs or to stay in their old ones, the resistance died.

Thus, resistance may be thoroughly justified because the proposed changes are harmful in some way. It may force one to think more carefully about introducing change. It is easier to handle resistance if you see it as functional, not as a challenge to your authority and your ideas. It helps to ask:

What useful purpose is the resistance serving?

If you expect there to be resistance this can become a self-fulfilling prophecy. Act, instead, as if people will respond to change in a variety of ways, both positively and negatively.

Coping with resistance

Since resistance is so common how should managers go about coping with it? The first step is to:

Identify real or perceived negative consequences of the change.

Having analysed what factors are contributing to resistance:

Weaken the apparent link between the change and the negative consequences.

People resist change because they see no personal pay-off and because they believe they, or something they value, will be adversely affected. Dealing with resistance means recognising this and taking appropriate action.

Experienced managers often assume that they cannot eliminate resistance and that the main aim must be to reduce it to manageable proportions. Take for example Alfred Turner, the manager in charge of a large, privately run, old people's home. He has three domestic cleaners on his staff and wants to alter the way that they organise their work so that one cleaner spends much of her time operating the laundry equipment. Two of the domestics will have to change the floor on which they work to make the plan succeed. He knows that they have become committed to working on their particular floor and take pride in the standard of cleanliness which they achieve. They will be reluctant to change to another floor.

Rather than simply instruct them and risk creating smouldering resentment he calls them together to discuss the problem. He shows them the total number of hours of cleaning available and the number of hours needed to run the laundry equipment and asks for their ideas. At first they sit back and look confused. With a bit more encouragement a lively discussion begins on ways of running the laundry equipment in a more sensible way than at present. Eventually one of the cleaners puts forward the plan Alfred already has in mind. There is no resistance.

Actions

You may often need to think in terms of actions to reduce rather than eliminate resistance. It may be avoided or at least reduced with these kinds of actions:

- avoid surprises. People need time to come to terms with change. Let people think about proposals and they will be less inclined to automatically resist them

- obtain top management support

- provide information. Lack of information creates a vacuum which will be filled with conjectures, rumours and assumptions leading to increased resistance; replace with knowledge, particularly about personal pay-offs from the change. Resisters may become allies

- ensure participation. Make your changes their changes by enabling those affected to:

    have a stake in the change

    feel that some or all of the change is their own, not devised and operated by outsiders

    help diagnose the problem and feel its importance

    reach a group consensus in support

- reduce, rather than increase, burdens. People will support changes which help them rather than add to their problems

- recognise feelings. It is essential to deal with the feelings aroused by a change which may threaten people in some way. Acknowledge valid objections and take steps to relieve unnecessary fears

- incorporate values and ideals. If what you propose accords with the values and ideals of those affected they will be less likely to oppose what you want to do

- offer new, worthwhile experiences

- avoid threats to autonomy and security

- be adaptable. Keep your project or plan open to revision or modification if experience suggests that alterations are desirable

- offer a neutral period: one during which employee work performance cannot adversely affect personal income or other benefits

- introduce new blood. New managers can often overcome resistance where older ones have failed. A new person has a good chance to sweep aside old ways of thinking and of doing things. The momentum may carry others along

- convince opinion-makers. Look for strategically placed people in pivotal positions and persuade them. They will carry others

- pay the price of change. Be willing to bear the risks inherent in creative innovation. If managers are put on the defensive about their ideas, are penalised or are not rewarded for risk taking they will not commit themselves to change

- set the stage for change. Managers should show a positive attitude to change and innovation, selling the idea of team effort; creating opportunities to learn and accept change

- simplicity. Keep the change simple to understand

- small steps. Introduce changes in small steps rather than one big one

- compatibility. Try making the change fit the organisational environment as far as possible

- timing. Avoid introducing change at an entirely inappropriate and inconvenient time such as Christmas or the New Year

- informal leaders. Involve the informal leaders since this gives the programme credibility

- avenues of appeal. Build into the change programme a formal route for appeal that eases upward communication from dissatisfied individuals.

This is not a comprehensive list of possible actions. As the Murdoch examples above showed it is also possible to adopt power strategies as a way of dealing with resistance. Coercion forces compliance and produces a low level of commitment to the change. However, in some cases managers may decide that compliance is all they require.

A longer-term strategy to deal with resistance to change is a re-education programme. This assumes that those on the receiving end are rational and will respond to facts and information, and is usually only feasible when change does not have to be immediate. Re-education can occur through extensive organisational development techniques, training and communication programmes and other information sharing methods. These usually start with establishing in everyone's mind a clear need for change. While re-education may prevent appeals to resist change from succeeding it is not a reliable way of achieving large-scale change in the short run, particularly where motivation to change is low.

Another approach to minimising resistance is through the technique of identification. You provide the people you want to influence with a living example of the behaviour which you want to promote. People learn by identifying with you and trying to be like you. For example, a manager who wants to encourage his subordinates to get closer to the customer has to be seen doing this too, spending time listening to what customers say and using the results to influence future actions.

By virtue of its existence, resistance brings people into conflict with managers wanting to make change. Handling conflict is therefore an important management skill. Managers deal with conflict in varying ways, the main ones being:

- *avoidance* – withdrawing from the conflict situation

- *smoothing* – trying to cover up and pretend that everything is calm, co-operative and pleasant

- *bargaining* – compromising, inviting negotiation; each part gains and each part loses or gives up something

- *forcing* – fighting a battle to see which party will be the winner; creates a win/lose situation

- *problem solving* – confronting the issue; implies collaborative working not fighting amongst parties to solve the problem.

The last of these tends to be most productive although, depending on the power situation, both forcing and bargaining can also be effective. See also Chapter 20 on Verbal Skills and Chapter 6 on Power and Influence.

Overcoming individual resistance

Although resistance can reflect the variety of factors discussed in this chapter, ultimately much of the resistance encountered in managing organisational change reflects individual concerns or anxieties. Research has indicated that, in the face of change, people tend to experience a range of emotions, and in consequence demonstrate a range of responses. Initial excitement or enthusiasm may quickly turn into fear and anxiety, and this in turn is often rapidly translated into denial or resistance. In this state of mind, individuals may then apply a range of stratagems to hinder the change process, ranging from apparently rational debate ('This is not going to work because . . .') through to simple obstruction or even sabotage.

One of the most common responses is simply to ignore the changes. When one local authority introduced a new set of processes in order to meet government requirements on competitive tendering, it found initially that employees simply disregarded these and continued to operate as before. When the authority tried to enforce the new arrangements, employees showed extraordinary ingenuity in their resistance – in some cases, actually operating two parallel systems in order to pay lip-service to the new while retaining the old. It was only when the authority redirected its efforts to changing employee attitudes, through direct interaction and communication, that the new processes were finally implemented.

The key lesson here is that, although it is possible, using the various techniques set out earlier in this chapter, to structure the overall change process in order to help overcome organisational resistance, it will also be necessary in most cases to work directly with the individuals who are affected in order to overcome their personal concerns and fears. These individuals may include the senior managers whose commitment and leadership is required, the middle managers and supervisors who will implement the changes, or the wider workforce who may be on the receiving end of whatever emerges.

Some of this intervention will be collective, applying the communication techniques outlined in Chapter 5. However, in many cases, there is no substitute for direct interaction with the individuals concerned, with a focus on reassurance, persuasion and consultation.

Influencing skills

Effective influencing requires a high level of personal skill, based on sensitivity both to the overall demands of the situation and to the specific needs or expectations of the individuals being persuaded. It is important to note that effective influencing is not about deviousness or deceit. Even if you succeed in pulling the wool over the eyes of the individual in question, this is not likely to produce long-term commitment to the outcomes of the change. Rather, influencing is about achieving an acceptance of the new situation on a basis that is acceptable to both parties – in effect, a form of negotiation.

Influencing styles vary, reflecting both the situation and the preferences and characteristics of the individuals involved. Typically, though, styles fall into two broad categories, which can be applied in a variety of permutations in order to achieve a practical outcome:

- push styles

- pull styles.

Push styles of influencing are essentially about assertion and focusing on your own agenda. They include stating clearly your own views and opinions, making clear your feelings or emotions about the subject, confirming your expectations or requirements of the other person, and – in extreme cases – applying incentives or potential threats. *Pull styles*, on the other hand, are about responsiveness and a willingness to focus on the other people's agendas. Approaches here may include active listening to their views, exploring their feelings or opinions, attempting to identify and build common ground, and openly expressing your own feelings in order to encourage the other person to express theirs.

There is no right or wrong approach among these various styles and their use will in part depend on your own role, characteristics and preferences. In general, some of us are comfortable being assertive, while others prefer to take a more responsive role. Moreover, we may need to adopt different styles in different circumstances. At a simple level, our approach to our boss may be different from our approach to our subordinates. Increasingly, too, in many organisations traditional authority relationships are being replaced by more fluid structures, which in turn require different styles of influencing. For example, the management of a multi-functional project team, whose members report formally to a range of different managers, will probably require the adoption of a pull style to ensure commitment to the project goals.

More generally, though, different situations will also require different styles. If there is a clear-cut need for a quick response to a situation it may be appropriate to adopt a very assertive style ('I want us to do this, and I want us to do it now . . .'), perhaps based on a clear statement of your views and requirements. If the issue is relatively 'cut and dried' you may simply need to communicate your reasons very clearly to the other parties and they will take action accordingly.

Where the situation is less straightforward, however, it may well be appropriate to adopt a more responsive approach. For example, if there are a variety of different options it may well be prudent to listen to different views before agreeing a course of action that all parties can accept. Most commonly, in the context of change, such views will be a mixture of rational argument and personal emotions or anxiety, and these different elements may, in practice, be hard to disentangle. Apparently logical arguments may simply disguise concerns based on personal fears. People are generally reluctant to admit that they are opposing change because, for instance, they fear they will not be able to cope or because they are afraid of having their own situation worsened. Instead, they will concoct a range of apparently good reasons why the changes are not in the best interests of the organisation as a whole.

In 'selling' change to others it is necessary to work through these different agendas in order to understand, as clearly as possible, the grounds of the other person's resistance. If you simply assume that the resistance is driven by self-interest you may overlook some genuine concerns about the nature of the proposed changes. Conversely, if you try to respond to every apparently reasoned objection you may find that you waste considerable time on what are, in essence, simply personal agendas.

Skilled change agents will initially identify those individuals who are likely to be key stakeholders in the change process, from senior management downwards. In practice, this group can be defined as any one who has the potential significantly to impede the change process. The handling of this group will depend on the numbers involved, but in general it is worth spending time face-to-face influencing such individuals.

Depending on the individual response, these sessions may vary from straightforward communication ('This is what we are proposing to do and why'), through consultation ('I'd welcome your views as to how we should handle this aspect'), to counselling ('I know you're unhappy with what we're proposing. Can we talk through your concerns?'). In practice, the skilled influencer will often use a range of styles in the course of the session, perhaps beginning by asserting his own views and then gradually adopting a more responsive approach in order to gain the other person's commitment.

Clearly, the counselling elements of this process need to be handled with some care. If you suspect that the individual has some personal fears or concerns about the change process, then your aim will be to encourage discussion of these without making the person feel threatened or patronised. This is where the 'pull' techniques are invaluable. Through careful and responsive listening to what the individual is saying you may well pick up clues or hints about the real areas of anxiety, which will enable you to explore further. If you are open about your own feelings and views, you will encourage the other person to behave similarly ('I know I've had some worries about the impact of that part of the change on me . . .What's your view on that?'). Another option is to generalise the topic under discussion so as to allow the individual to voice his or her concerns, in effect, in the third-person ('I get the impression that a lot of people are concerned about the effects of this. Do you think any of your people are worried?').

Through these kind of sessions, it is possible to begin to build up an understanding of the nature of individual concerns or anxieties. This will provide you with an indication of how to apply some of the techniques set out in this chapter to help overcome resistance generally. Perhaps more importantly, however, at an individual level you can start to talk through with people their concerns about the process. In some cases, the very act of talking about the concerns may itself help people to come to terms with them. Furthermore, people are often reassured simply by the knowledge that their fears or concerns are not unique but are shared by others. More commonly, though, the discussion will enable you to identify some common ground or compromise position, which will meet the change objectives while also addressing the concerns raised.

In general terms, even if it is not possible to address all concerns, ultimate commitment to the change process will generally be much stronger if individuals feel that their views have been taken into account along the way. Even if it is possible to respond in only a limited way to the views and concerns expressed this may often be of immense symbolic value in 'selling' the end process. For example, in one company undergoing major structural changes, it became clear in discussions with middle managers that proposed changes in job titles were seen as reducing their perceived status. Although this was clearly a relatively trivial matter in the face of the changes taking place it was seen as a 'last straw' by some managers, who were already having to cope with significantly increased workload and responsibilities. By abandoning this comparatively minor proposed change the organisation gained substantially increased commitment to the wider changes from the managers involved.

GUIDELINES

- *Identify* if possible the type of resistance you expect to meet: cultural; social; organisational; psychological

- *Analyse* resistance by: intensity; source; and focus

- *Look* for behavioural factors, such as emotional reasons for resistance, and rational or system factors

- *View* resistance to organisational change as perfectly rational rather than irrational

- *Ask* what useful purpose the resistance is serving

- *Identify* real or perceived negative consequences of the change, then

- *Weaken* the apparent link between the change and the negative consequences

- *Reduce* rather than eliminate resistance by measures such as avoiding surprises; obtaining top management support for the change; providing information; participation; and so on

- *Work* directly with the individuals who are affected in order to overcome their personal concerns and fears

- *Use* a mixture of 'push' and 'pull' styles to influence individual behaviour and opinions, depending on the situation and the personality of the individual concerned.

8   Planning strategic change

When, some years ago, John Welch became chairman of General Electric (GE) in the USA, the first thing he did was to dismantle most of the company's strategic planning department. A review of the last 20 years revealed that each of GE's major internally grown business successes stemmed from outside the strategic planning system. Similarly, the failure of Videotext, one of the most heavily researched business projects of recent years, shows that research and a sophisticated planning process are no panacea.

Change-minded organisations set direction not detailed strategy. They realise that forecasting is full of surprises and that more relevant than planning is being well informed and ready to grab opportunities when they come their way, which is often. Another major difference between change-minded organisations and others is that strategy is not divorced from implementation. The two are built together, the strategy and beginning to make it happen. It is not planning in a vacuum, with someone dreaming up the future and other people then figuring out how to make it happen.

There are two main kinds of planned change:

- strategic

- operational.

Operational change is about making improvements, in the short or sometimes long term, based on rapid response and adaptation. It is day-to-day change with which all managers are familiar. Chance plays a big part in deciding what and when change can occur. This type of planned change is opportunity change. The scope for systematic planning is usually limited. For instance, when the stock market crashed in November 1987 this had been predicted for more than a year. The Australian Robert Holmes à Court, who made his name holding company shares until someone else needed them for a takeover bid, found his assets worth far less than he had originally paid for them. Whether he went broke or not was one of the questions that fascinated observers at the time. Though Holmes could afford the best investment and planning support available it did him little good because, even if it rightly predicted the crash, what counted more was the opportunism of acting at just the right moment.

Strategic change deals with large-scale strategic alternatives. It is about major shifts in one or more of the main elements of any organisation:

- technical system – fitting resources to aims; fitting people to roles; measuring performance, staffing and development

- political system – who gets to influence things; distribution and balance of power across groups; managing succession politics; reward systems

- cultural system – aligning culture with mission and strategy; forming an organisational culture; managing rewards to shape the culture; selection of people to build or reinforce culture.

These ultimately decide an organisation's market share, its ability to innovate, to develop, change and survive. You can think of these three main components of strategic change as strands of a rope, hard to see from a distance yet clear when you come up close. Handling planned strategic change takes account of all three systems that make up the organisation (See Chapter 1 on Models).

Strategic planning is the point at which leaders enter, a new definition of the situation is made and a description of the future created which lifts the experiments of innovators from the periphery to centre stage. The activities of pioneers, mavericks, the 'product champions' and outsiders are given a new place in the sun, their ideas cease being irrelevant and become the way forward.

Formal planning systems contribute to major change; they seldom generate it. Breakthrough ideas stem from elsewhere, such as outside factors, special studies, ideas from existing developments, the drive and vision of inspired people who want to change the world. These ideas are incorporated into plans preserving the illusion that the planning process works. Detailed strategic plans are frequently afterthoughts cloaking emotions and intuitions with an aura of sober judgement. Creating the plan is often far more important than the plan itself. It is a way of clarifying 'where we want to be', and as such is concerned with direction.

Plans dealing with new methods, products, services, and structures are important, though not always for the reasons that people think. They are symbols, advertisements which attract investors, games used to test people's commitment to ideas and they are a justification for taking action. It is easy to be blinded by the planning process, seeing the creation of a plan as a substitute for action – the paralysis of analysis. Action not plans leads to management success.

The planning process is about sharing vision, expectations, understandings and information. Thus it is a communication tool which can contribute to people working together better. Most strategic plans are notable in retrospect for what they did not include and judged solely on their predictive powers they are usually dismal failures. Their merit is in helping managers to communicate to each other, to employees, to shareholders and others where the organisation is heading.

The planners

Strategic change has so many different variables that it does not readily lend itself to quantitative techniques or even formal analysis. Strategic planning relying on extensive documentation and elaborate research is symbolised by the rise and fall of the corporate planner. In the 20-year period to the mid-1970s corporate planning promised managers a convincing way to create the future. Reports bulging with forecasts and indicators of performance were the rage.

Organisations vied to produce volumes of figures, policy statements and strategic goals. The producers of these imaginative documents worked in a financial and economic climate where they could virtually make their forecasts occur. But by the late 1970s and 1980s the climate had changed, and it became apparent that the planners and forecasters were not so talented after all.

Enterprises which are deeply committed to long-term formalised planning systems tend to react to outside events slowly because they are locked into expensively created predictions. People are loath to say that the vision of the future is wrong.

Contrary to the commonly held notion of how managers should act, at the strategic level managerial leaders avoid elaborate packages of goals since this can:

- *suggest* that the issue is closed for discussion or debate

- *cut* people off from useful information

- *focus* opposition

- *cause* rigidity; fixed goals are hard to alter – people's egos are involved

- *offer* hostages to fortune

- *damage* security; good people may leave the organisation taking secrets with them.

Box 14

Benefits of formal planning systems

- Push people periodically to look ahead

- Stimulate vigorous communications about goals, strategic issues and resource allocations

- Prompt longer-term or more detailed analysis than would otherwise occur

- Lengthen time horizons and thus protect long-term investments such as research and development

- Provide a psychological backdrop and information framework about the future against which short-term decisions can be calibrated

- Fine-tune existing commitments

- Help implement strategic change once this has been decided upon

---

It is more accurate to see strategic planning as a series of smaller decisions made over time which evolve into major change. It may be hard to identify a single strategic plan that has momentous implications. For example, the decision by General Motors in America to produce smaller cars was not originally contained in a single plan. It came from a number of turning points.

So what use are formal planning systems? Their main contribution is providing support for making choices about how the future might look. They offer benefits such as those shown in Box 14. Even with formal planning, change is messy, involving an erratic path of learning and developing ideas.

Incrementalism versus the radical shift

The urgency faced by many major and medium-sized organisations to change in order to survive places a premium on fast, radical change. The idea of the transforming leader, the manager who inspires and shakes the entire organisation, is a reflection of the pressures for change which exist throughout the industrial world.

An impatience to make things happen is increasingly reflected in the tenure of managers who seldom stay more than a few years in their job and hence need to produce results in a hurry. There is an apparent divide between those organisations and their leaders who see strategic planning as a constant process of staying flexible, visionary, and radical, and those where change is preferred as a more incremental, step-by-step process.

The split between the incremental approach and the transforming one is a false division. There are many elements of incrementalism which the rapidly changing organisation must adopt. Similarly, those which rely on the incremental approach must often accept a large amount of change that from many viewpoints is radical.

Incrementalism has been called iterative and criticised as 'muddling through'. Yet this is how many of the world's most successful organisations operate. Strategic planning is not simply muddling through, nor is it an exercise of power or the use of formal planning systems:

Change strategies emerge from a series of subsystems which themselves may be highly rational. It is the total approach which is incremental.

Subsystems may deal in a highly disciplined way with specific issues such as acquisitions, market diversifications, structural change, and so on. Or strategic planning can be focused on important new organisational groupings such as in Pepsi Cola, where people are put in charge of managing 16-ounce returnable bottles, merchandising, convenience stores and so on. Cohesion arises from combining a rigorous approach with judgement, intuition and flair.

Despite criticisms of incrementalism as either too slow or muddled it can be: purposeful; effective; and proactive. Major organisational change is usually handled incrementally because strategic change has its own timing and driving forces. Managers need time to think through new roles, decide who can do what, assess individual reactions, develop solutions to new problems and so on.

Incrementalism is the essential thread that links:

- information gathering

- analysis

- testing

- behaviour

- power considerations.

Unlike the preparation of a fine banquet, it is impossible for even a visionary managerial leader to orchestrate all internal decisions, external environmental events, behaviour and power relationships, technical and information needs so that at any precise moment they join coherently.

By developing broad-brush statements of the desired future incrementalism assists by making results realistic and attainable. Strategic plans are the springboard from which management action is launched. They do not simply come from managers' heads, but involve input and influence from people inside and beyond the immediate organisation. There must normally be some sense of shared vision about the future around which detailed plans are constructed and actions agreed.

A road map

There is no system to guarantee strategic change. Planning mechanisms, project teams or sophisticated matrix structures all assume that the task is like drawing a correct wiring diagram. There may be no single solution because of conflicting interests within:

- the organisational hierarchy

- the different operational units of the organisation.

With hierarchical structures, communications travel up and down usually without skipping levels, making it slow to develop plans and providing plenty of room for errors and misunderstandings about what is being attempted. With few operating levels and many autonomous units, it is hard to tie all the segments into a coherent strategy with a clear sense of direction.

Planning strategic change is like creating a road map of where you want to go, marking out the main routes, not compiling a manual of instructions for how to get there. It hardly matters whether the plan is accurate; it is more important that there is some attempt to visualise and influence the future. The three elements common to all planning approaches are:

- *diagnosis* – choosing the desired end state

- *planning* – how to handle the transition state

- *interventions* – actions to move towards the end state.

(See Figure 2 in Chapter 1 on Models.)

Defining the future and how to get there is concerned with stating the fields of activity in which the organisation is going to excel. Interventions are about implementation and it is this area of change management that until recently has been relatively neglected, often in favour of time spent on bureaucratic systems for deciding direction and devising strategy.

Deciding on the end state

In essence you are trying to answer the question:

If we succeed, what will the end state be like?

The end state describes in terms of a battle where the organisation will be. For commercial concerns it is the battle to compete and win. For public and voluntary agencies it is the battle to offer service users maximum choice and quality of service.

Competitive strategies must enable the company to achieve strategic superiority. This is managed either through: occupying a distinct place in the marketplace via quality, image, distribution or innovation; or through achieving low production costs relative to competitors.

Public-service strategies must enable the agency to be either highly responsive to user needs; or to use resources so cost effectively that a relative lack of flexibility is accepted.

In striving towards a new end state, organisations will implement their strategies so as to affect structures, policies, authority, tasks, styles, roles, and so on. Since organisations do not stop developing, it may not be obvious when the new state has been reached. Occasionally, when the end state is visualised in numerical terms, it is easier to decide the outcome. However, this is seldom motivating enough to sustain an organisation through its many ups and downs on the way to the desired end state.

In order to define a vision of the end state some organisations use outside consultants while others use their formal planning system, and still others rely on leadership qualities. No matter how it is done there must be decisions about:

- How big a change are we talking about?
  How different will the end state be from the present one?

- How fast will we move towards the end state?
  A wrong choice about the timescale can threaten an organisation's survival. Major change condensed into two to three years means that the period will be an unstable one; major change spread over three to five years means that during this time the organisation will

be in a transitional phase; finally, a major change spread over five or more years means that the organisation is essentially always stable.

• What is the likely impact of the changes for achieving the end state?

In answering these questions managerial leaders will be moving towards defining a position in which the organisation has a position of strategic excellence. Cuno Pumpin, Professor of Business Administration at St Gallen, one of the leading business schools of Europe, defines a strategic excellence position (SEP) as:

a capability which enables an organisation to produce better than average results over the long term compared to its competitors.

Planning strategic change aims to identify and move the organisation to occupy strategic excellence positions.

The SEP concept has assisted international companies such as Audi, Ciba and Geigy. There are some basic rules which have major ramifications for planning change (see Box 15). They concentrate energy, thought, and ultimately resources – just as a magnifying glass focuses the sun until it creates a fire.

Box 15

Ten laws of strategic excellence positions

1 The existence of SEPs determine a company's success

2 SEPs are developed by the allocation of resources

3 The resources allocated to a given SEP must be withdrawn from other possible SEPs, unless there is synergy between them

4 The number of SEPs that can be developed is limited

5 Once an SEP has been developed it can be maintained only if it is constantly nurtured by the allocation of appropriate resources

6 SEPs may stand in a harmonious, neutral or conflicting relation to each other

7 Strong SEPs can only be developed if all the company's specialist managers are involved in interdisciplinary cooperation

8 Developing SEPs is a medium- to long-term strategy

9 The benefits of SEPs change over time

10 There is a close relation between a company's corporate culture and its SEPs

---

Source: The Essence of Corporate Strategy, C Pumpin, Aldershot, Gower, 1987

The transition state

A major difference between planned and operational change is the need to plan for the transition state. With opportunity change the impact of the transition stage may be relatively small. But for strategic change you need to:

- *recognise* that the transition state is significantly different from the end state

- *make* separate plans for handling it

- *pay* particular attention to detecting blocks

- *tolerate* behaviour or action which reflects people's difficulty in adapting to new arrangements.

The London Borough of Croydon decided that it needed a new direction for its services to adults. The aim was to create better services and also balance a steadily growing bias towards children's services absorbing a disproportionate share of resources.

To promote the change it wanted all existing services for adults to be concentrated into a single operational division. However, full implementation lasted nearly two years and the benefits did not appear for some time. Meanwhile existing services had to be maintained. At the start of the transitional period the senior management developed a phased plan for moving into the new structure, providing opportunities within work teams for discussion and communication about the changes. Managing the transition stage was more complex and stressful than the eventual end state.

Thus the transition state is a distinctly different one from the desired end state and may require its own separate plan of action. Because this interim stage is often turbulent and stressful, attention must be paid to how the plan is progressing and to detecting blocks to progress. Many sensible plans fail because of insufficient attention to what is happening during the transition phase.

Devising a strategy

Since there is no science of strategic change there are many views on how actually to achieve strategic shifts:

- appeal to common sense

- re-educate people

- use power.

Common sense. This approach to strategic change relies on people being rational and acting sensibly, once they see their own self-interest. Believing this, you would concentrate on communicating the proposed changes clearly, showing the gains involved and assume that people will be sensible, motivated and follow your lead.

Re-education. This approach assumes that, even though the change you are planning is strategic, people will only understand it on a personal level in which what matters is how they see their world, their attitudes, values, skills and significant relationships. Knowledge and information are not enough. Believing this, you would plan strategic change by helping people to understand and cope with their future through, for example, training, career development, job redesign, redefining roles and so on.

Use of power. This approach says that people with less power comply with the plans, direction and leadership of those with greater power. Believing this you would select actions which emphasise what people must do, when they are to do it and who ensures that they do it.

While change may stem from a mixture of all three approaches, managers tend consciously or unconsciously to subscribe to one rather than another. What view you hold determines your change strategy. Review to what extent you are biased too much in favour of one particular approach.

Regardless of your particular preference you will need to engage in a purposeful and politically astute process. The crudities of management by objectives or narrow goal-setting are seldom enough. To devise a viable plan there are several elements to consider, as shown in Box 16.

Box 16

The elements of strategic planning

- Sense needs
- Build awareness
- Broaden support
- Create commitments
- Focus developments
- Seek accountability
- Maintain the dynamic

Sense needs

Deciding on major organisational change requires the instinct of a bloodhound, sniffing out areas where change is required. The evidence may be found in market research ratings, profit centres, the relationship between the organisation and its distributors, in technological developments, in what teams say, in a stream of unexpected problems and so on. There are many formal tools for detecting where and when strategic change is needed, and though initially the targets will be vague and ill-defined, gradually it becomes clearer what must be changed and how.

Vision plays a large part in sensing needs. Many organisations have been built on an unwavering vision of what the future would look like and what is needed. The power of that early vision can make market research, analysis and other planning techniques a distraction.

Build awareness

Demonstrating a need for major change is an essential part of evolving a strategy. There must be a level of common awareness in the organisation that a major change is now required. For instance, at Pepsi Cola one time president John Sculley wanted to invest in larger regional groups of independent bottlers. However, most of the available resources were being siphoned off into the new fast-food businesses and he concluded that there would be no general awareness of the need he had highlighted until these other businesses had succeeded.

Generating enough 'comfort' for the idea of strategic change may demand more than study groups, debates, seminars, surveys and so on. It will also need political skill in generating a will to listen to what may sometimes prove to be unpleasant or hard truths.

Broaden support

As awareness of the need for strategic change spreads, there are usually many informal discussions probing positions and challenging assumptions. At this stage it is essential not to lose patience with the sceptics and doubters. Adopting a new strategic direction challenges the *status quo* and many existing vested interests. There may be whole layers of people who find it easier to say no rather than yes, to pour cold water on ideas rather than encourage them.

The way forward is to seek constructive movement within the organisation without initially threatening major power centres. For example, discuss proposals in principle with the promise that details will be re-presented. Goals remain broad and unrefined.

Create commitments

It is rare that everyone who matters in an organisation agrees on the need for major change or how to achieve it. Create pockets of commitment to new directions, while projects are explored and options are kept open. This will mean being opportunistic about building small, isolated commitments into a more powerful force – to generate critical mass.

Focus developments

As the nature of the strategic goals crystallise, they must be channelled into specific proposals. For example, a crucial committee can help educate and neutralise opposition. At this stage goals begin to be quantified with outline timetables and costs. This is also the stage when marginal proposals are dropped.

Seek accountability

With the firming up of goals more people have to be made accountable for specific results. For example, it must be clear who does what, by when and with what resources. A useful way to clarify accountability is to state 'who owns' the responsibility for seeing that the plan becomes action.

Maintain the dynamic

Many strategic change efforts, after starting well, fizzle out. The art of strategic planning is to develop ways to maintain the momentum over a prolonged period which may stretch into years. Relying on many people to sustain the strategic change effort is better than relying on just a few individuals. Similarly, it may be sensible to pile change upon change so as to ensure the pressure behind the strategic shift is perpetuated. Also by having an 'owner' for ensuring that the plan happens there is an improved chance that the dynamic of change will be watched and if necessary action taken to maintain it.

GUIDELINES

- *Clarify* whether you are planning for strategic or operational change

- *Action* not plans lead to management success

- *Avoid* elaborate packages of goals

- *Base* plans on a shared vision about the future

- *Use* the main elements of strategic planning as shown in Box 16

- *Obtain* constructive movement within the organisation without initially threatening major power centres

- *Leave* goals broad and unrefined in the early stages of strategic planning

- *Create* pockets of commitment to new directions

- *Determine* who 'owns' the responsibility for pursuing strategic change

- *Develop* ways to sustain the momentum of the strategic change

- *Clarify* what the final end state will be like; how big a change we are talking about; and how different the end state will be from the present one

- *Make* separate plans for handling the transition state

- *Decide* how quickly the strategic change will occur.

9 Action-sequencing

The staff were all anxious. The ailing UK retail concern had been bought from its American parent by a new British board. Did the change disguise an asset-stripping programme? Could the new team turn the ship around?

For years the company which was rich in assets and people had been poor on results and profits. The new management's main concern was to win staff support and gain commitment to a new strategy. To assess part of the problem an attitude survey was conducted amongst the 20,000 employees who nearly all replied. Their message was clear:

- fear existed at all levels

- management meant 'I tell, you do'

- customers were seen as a threat

- communications were generally poor

- bureaucracy was rife.

Management were treated like clerks, being conditioned to handle systems, procedures, stock and property. People were to be manipulated and disciplined. Creativity and initiative had neither been expected nor rewarded. The survey results indicated a heartfelt cry from all staff to return pride and confidence in working for Woolworths. Fundamental perceptions had to be changed about what it meant to manage people. The behaviour of a great many people had to be modified.

To get action the top management decided to send a signal across the company: management means doing things right, leadership means doing the right things (see also Chapter 2 on Leadership). All 1,200 managers were to be given training spread over three years. The first year would emphasise leadership and the team; the second leadership and the customer; and the third leadership and the business. The aim was to revitalise leadership skills, sharpen awareness of customers and improve managers' perceptions of the entire business, not just their own part of it.

As a result of trials the stores' management structure and how they looked inside were changed. There was more emphasis on personal responsibility, more scope for the development of teams and freer, more open communication. The overall results of Woolworths Holdings, bolstered by strategic takeovers, improved from a £6 million profit in 1982 to a spectacular £115 million in 1986–7.

Although this is an old example, rejuvenating Woolworths was a classic case of major organisational change. It is possible to see in the process logical steps which are common to all large-scale organisational change efforts. The main action steps are those shown in Box 17 (see also Figure 2, page 7).

Box 17

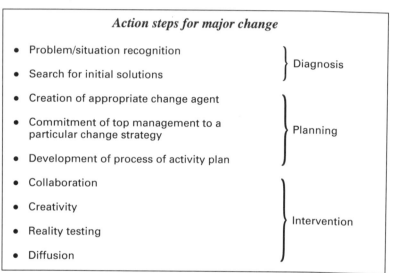

Action steps for major change

- Problem/situation recognition
- Search for initial solutions
} Diagnosis

- Creation of appropriate change agent
- Commitment of top management to a particular change strategy
- Development of process of activity plan
} Planning

- Collaboration
- Creativity
- Reality testing
- Diffusion
} Intervention

Problem/situation recognition

The start of handling change is to find out what needs doing. This involves scanning the environment, looking both inside and beyond the organisation, diagnosing the type of change required, assessing the direction, rate and magnitude of change needed. From these investigations strategies are developed.

While often presented as a logical, systematic process it is far more an intuitive one. Systematic analysis highlights problems and situations; the more thorough the study, the longer the list of things to do.

The managerial leadership task is to produce a list of priorities requiring intensive effort. Discovering what is happening and what must be done means leaving your desk and seeing for yourself. A study conducted by Professor Revans some years ago indicated that the most important issue for workers in several factories was the extent to which they felt that the management listened to them. Listening is a key skill at this stage (see also Chapters 15–20 on techniques).

Simplify issues by focusing on one or two main problems rather than half a dozen or more. Pick the fundamental and primary issues, not secondary concerns. Only by doing this can you create a momentum for a common view of the situation. Before action can be formulated convincingly most of the key people in the team or the organisation must also hold this view. No matter how complicated the situation, the areas in which change will occur reduce to those shown in Box 18.

Box 18

The focus for change	
• Impact on people • Decision process • External environment • Power groupings and aims of policy makers	Political
• Structure • Technology and use of techniques • Tasks being done • Regulatory systems	Technical
• Climate of the organisation • Norms and values • Staff qualities	Cultural

As there is often a wide divergence in how priorities are perceived across the organisation, it may be necessary to conduct goal setting exercises to identify new directions and specific targets for action. Goal setting exercises bring together key personnel who help list the issues within the overall problem statement and then work together to define ways of tackling them. Alternatively, the job may become one for a special project group reporting back to senior management.

Search for initial solutions

Faced with a complex situation requiring change a common management reaction is 'Where do I begin?' Successful change efforts suggest that change should start at those points in the system where some stress and strain exist, but not where these are the greatest. Strain causes dissatisfaction with the *status quo* and thus becomes a motivating factor for change in the system. Look carefully at the recipients of the proposed changes, to see if they can be grouped or segmented so as to benefit from slightly varying change strategies?

Stagnating organisations develop many layers of filters to keep out the external world. One solution may be to deliberately introduce conflict. This can stimulate the creation of mutual goals and values, integrating individuals into groups. Confrontation meetings, for example, can ensure that problems are aired along with alternative solutions.

Problems recognition narrows the task, putting crucial not marginal issues on the agenda for action. At this stage you are only looking for an outline of possible action and this must reflect:

- available resources

- an acceptable timescale.

It is no use, for example, devising a major change programme which cannot be properly financed. Similarly, there is no point planning a major change programme lasting too long.

At this early stage in the process of organising the change effort you should also identify how much commitment to change exists. The retailer's survey, for example, revealed that there was widespread staff support for it:

**The smaller the commitment, the more intense
the change effort required.**

Now is also the time to begin developing some criteria for judging the impact, the success or failure of any change. The short-term criterion may well be profits for a commercial concern or a service offering more consumer choice in the case of a public agency. The longer term is represented by the vision which managerial leaders develop. There will be many indicators of performance available. For example, once Apple Computer had begun making profits again in 1986, the change targets selected for one year onwards were 50,000 Macintosh sales a month, 50 per cent greater profit margins and a stock price of $50 a share. Some possible criteria for judging solutions are shown in Box 19.

Box 19

Checklist for judging solutions

- What are the relative advantages, ie unique benefits of change?
- What will be the impact on social relations?
- To what extent can the situation be reversed if change occurs and we want to go back?
- How complex and difficult to understand will the change be?
- How well does the change fit in with other aspects such as group values, beliefs, norms etc?
- What is the appropriate rate of change – introduce it slowly or quickly?
- What risks or uncertainties are involved?
- What commitment is required to implement and sustain change?

In formulating solutions it is also sensible to consider:

How secure is it to undertake change?

This means looking at how individuals are feeling and the organisational factors making it unsafe to tackle situations, such as perceived likely success or failure of change, confidence, self-esteem, culture climate, etc. Any major change has a ripple effect and cannot be neatly confined to one part of the enterprise. For example, to change behaviour at one level of a hierarchical organisation it is necessary to achieve complementary and reinforcing changes both above and below this level. Reviewing safety and how people are feeling determines whether to phase in the changes or use the big bang approach.

As the retailer experience underlines, formulating a major change demands attention to organisational norms. These are the hidden values influencing how change will be received and managed. If an organisation has long held beliefs, traditions, and a history of minimal change, some formal process may be needed to unfreeze attitudes and behaviour. The retailer tackled this by creating an 'Excellence programme' for store staff which, in parallel to the leadership programme for managers, offered rewards, recognitions for achievement and progress towards a standard or personal and team achievement. Other ways of unfreezing attitudes also exist, such as confrontation meetings, project groups, education programmes, and so on.

A common mistake often made at this early stage in deciding how to handle change is to have a favourite idea about how to tackle the situation. For instance some managers always restructure, others always improve communications, others replace people and yet others focus on production and control systems. It is important to avoid being 'solution minded' and imposing ways of tackling situations which are not actually needed. A fear of being thought indecisive sometimes causes insufficient time and effort to be spent on reviewing the choices.

Another common mistake is thinking that management's main role is exhorting and selling the change. Advocating change, however, is no guarantee of movement. Similarly, although problem analysis may quickly reveal what needs doing, the next step is not necessarily to announce what will happen next. Many major changes can be achieved almost imperceptibly and can influence thinking throughout the enterprise without a big announcement. In fact, the Japanese often criticise Western managers for 'Announcementitis', that is, rushing to make public statements about proposed solutions, which creates resistance.

Create appropriate change agent

Change agents are the catalysts for making things happen, precipitating and often leading the change effort. They may be existing managers, project teams, a representative group charged with a task, a team of consultants from elsewhere in the organisation, specialists recruited from outside, and sometimes the entire staff group.

Selecting a change agent is important to ensure that the change strategy happens. The responsibility for 'ownership' of the change effort must be identified as it will be hard to switch horses once the race for change has begun. Since major change may take years to implement there needs to be some continuity in ownership of the change effort. This is why a chairman, managing director or senior member of the managing board of an organisation is often selected to lead the change.

A popular change agent in recent years has been the corporate entrepreneur or product champion. The latter has a high need for achievement and visibility and fights hard for a particular organisational change because they identify their own personal success with it. The change agent can thus be selected from a variety of different people or groups. What matters is choosing one that is appropriate to the change required and ensuring long-term continuity.

Commitment to a particular change strategy

People will accept a general aim and argue endlessly about the specifics. At this stage the central issue is 'How will we manage the change?' not

'What objectives shall we set?' It is more important to have:

- a clear sense of direction

- a description of the desired end state after the change

- full commitment by senior management to the proposed way of achieving the end state.

In order to gain senior management commitment it is better to have general goals, as opposed to highly specific, measurable or quantitative ones. These general goals help to promote cohesion; they make people feel comfortable with the idea of change; create identity and a sense of common well-being; and promote creative problem solving.

Managers responsible for achieving major change over a lengthy period may have difficulty in obtaining the backing of top management since it is often hard to demonstrate convincingly that the results are achievable, and are the best use of resources. For example, there may be pressure to put the resources to more immediate productive use, such as spending them on advertising, than investing in research and development. Unless top management are behind the broadly defined change programme and involved in seeing that it happens, the chances of a major change effort succeeding are much reduced. Many organisations that have launched programmes to improve the quality of their products with only token top management commitment have inevitably run out of steam.

Finally, commitment to the chosen change agent is also required. The latter must have ready access to top management to report and discuss how the change effort is going and whether further help is needed to keep it moving.

Develop process or activity plan

This stage converts 'How will we manage the process of change?' into a detailed map of the change effort. There are now more specific aims which can be broken down into a variety of detailed tasks to be performed. Since every organisation is unique there can be no precise definition of an effective development process or activity plan, but the features of such a plan are suggested below.

A strategic plan which does not lead to action is not much use. It must also be sufficiently different from what has happened in the past to be setting a new direction. In judging its likely effectiveness people will expect to understand how one action relates to another. Thus, for example, in the retailer's training programme the company knew how the first year's programme led into the second and then into the third and how they all tied into a single overall aim.

An effective activity plan can be scheduled and the main staging posts identified without going into great detail. This means specifying who does what to whom by when. The use of networks and critical path techniques are sometimes helpful at this stage.

Any plan for handling major change must also be capable of being adapted to meet unexpected situations. The more detailed the aims the harder it will be to modify in new situations, so it is usually preferable to keep the plan simple and have a range of contingency plans which respond to some of the more important 'what if . . .' situations.

It is worth considering creating a separate path for handling the transition state – those dynamic stages the organisation will go through in order to reach the desired end state. Since the latter can be months or even years away there is often a need for temporary structures or arrangements. Most of the stresses arising from the change effort will certainly be in evidence during the transition state which therefore justifies a plan of its own if the change is a large one.

To steer the transition stage it may be sensible to create a separate structure, such as having a senior manager to handle and coordinate it; a project manager reporting to the board; the use of existing members of the hierarchy; a special group drawn from those subsections of the organisation that will be affected by the change; natural leaders; a representative sample from each part of the organisation; reliable colleagues and so on.

Whoever handles the transition state must have authority to keep it moving, command the respect of top management and front-line employees and possess good interpersonal skills. Whatever the temporary system, if it is to work well it must be properly communicated to everyone, and understood.

You cannot make a complete plan for change. There is no science of organisation change and the more senior you are in the organisation the more you will lack vital information which is held elsewhere and usually lower down in the organisation. Focus on direction and keeping up the momentum of the plan.

Collaboration

Not every manager experienced in handling large-scale change agrees on the importance of collaboration. Some believe in using management power to force change with or without support from those affected. Others feel that collaboration is essential if the change is to work properly. Studies of successful change efforts suggest that it pays to identify those subsystems primarily involved in the change and to build a commitment through participation in problem solving and discussion.

Commitment comes from genuinely seeking suggestions for action and using these where appropriate. To be seen as responsive to ideas you may need to encourage the involvement of people who appear opposed to the plans. The benefits of this are:

● opponents often insert reality into management thinking about what is feasible

● those outside formal decision centres often underestimate the difficulty of achieving change; by encouraging them to participate they will often become more realistic.

Collaboration sounds a vague idea; in practice it simply means working with those subsystems vital to the change effort to create a realistic plan (see also Chapter 4 on Commitment). Collaboration in making the planned change will occur when some or all of the conditions shown in Box 20 exist. (See also Chapter 12 on Participative Decision-Making.)

Box 20

Conditions for collaborating with planned change

● People feel pressure to change and participate in designing it

● Early changes bring tangible results and are limited in scope

● Change is spread throughout the organisation, affecting many people and producing positive benefits in terms of attitudes

● People are helped to behave more effectively in solving problems and relating to each other

● There is an improved organisational performance

Creativity

Planning and implementing change depends on creativity. As plans turn into more detailed tasks there is the opportunity and indeed the need to question old ways and to acknowledge that they may no longer be effective. For many people the exciting and attractive aspect of change is that it introduces new ways of thinking, working and doing.

Whether in the shape of innovative new products or new groupings of resources, creativity offers scope for people to express their personality and skills.

The creativity for precipitating major organisation change is sometimes crushed by the inertia of the old ways and existing commitments. Organisations have tried many approaches for releasing the creative energies that undoubtedly reside within the enterprise. Much depends on the prevailing culture and particularly leadership as to whether genuinely new ways of doing and thinking will emerge.

You can assess the climate for creativity in your own organisation by examining how the so-called 'odd-balls' are treated. These are the mavericks, the rebels and people who are often labelled as 'difficult'. The history of successful innovation and change is replete with how such individuals have seen what others have refused to see and against heavy odds have eventually been influential in forcing the necessary organisation shifts.

Change brings the ideas of those on the periphery to the centre stage. Minority views, struggling projects, 'strange ideas' suddenly become respectable as the organisation shifts direction. Thus, during the change process the management task is to encourage creativity in new ways of thinking that will enable the change plans to work. For this to occur there must be a climate of tolerance for exploring new possibilities and for testing out previously dismissed ideas.

Reality-testing

Many aspects of large-scale organisational changes may first need testing on a small scale to see whether underlying ideas and solutions work. This is equivalent to test marketing a product in one part of the country before launching it nationally. Often top management decides that it simply has no time for this luxury and must risk the change without reality-testing. It is, however, worth testing both the readiness and capability of subsystems to change. Launching a major change programme which assumes a general willingness to respond and then meets major resistance may delay for years the achievement of real change.

An obvious area where reality-testing is sensible is when management is relying on training to produce important results. There needs to be some evidence that the proposed training plan will indeed contribute as expected to the change effort before it is used on a big scale involving many employees.

Diffusion

Diffusion is concerned with follow through – seeing that agreed and sometimes tested changes permeate the organisation. This is one of the weakest areas of handling change and the one which is least well researched.

It is important for management to monitor whether the required changes are actually taking place and according to the agreed timetable. This follow-up is hard work and many managers find it the least creative and congenial of the steps required for producing major change. Lack of diffusion, caused by a failure to monitor, explains why perfectly sensible change plans sometimes fail (see Chapter 14 on Tracking).

GUIDELINES

- *Look* inside and beyond the organisation to determine the change situation

- *Listen* to learn about changes needed

- *Use* goal setting exercises to help determine change requirements

- *List* priorities to focus intensive effort on change

- *Start* the change effort where some stress and strain exist, not where these are the greatest

- *Consider* creating mutual goals and values through introducing conflict

- *Make* action plans reflect available resources and an acceptable timescale

- *Develop* criteria for judging the impact of planned change

- *Review* how individuals are feeling and factors that may make it unsafe to tackle situations

- *Avoid* being solution minded

- *Beware* of 'announcementitis'

- *Decide* who 'owns' the responsibility for the change effort

- *Gain* senior management commitment in the early stages of planned change by having general rather than highly specific goals

- *Schedule* the planned changes to clarify who does what and when

- *Consider* creating a separate plan for handling the transition state

- *Focus* on direction and keeping up the momentum of the plan

- *Build* commitment through participation in problem solving and discussion

- *Assess* the climate for creativity in your own organisation by examining how the mavericks are treated

- *Promote* tolerance for exploring new possibilities, for testing previously dismissed ideas

- *Test* the readiness of subsystems to change and their capability of doing so.

10 Project management techniques

Those who are experienced in managing large-scale organisational change tend to have a wide range of myths and cautionary tales about the challenges of making change happen. One project manager, working in a large organisation, had a series of old sepia photographs on the wall behind his desk. The first, taken from an old newspaper, showed two halves of a nearly completed bridge missing one another by nearly a metre. The project manager had added the caption 'Poor Co-ordination.' Another showed a train that had crashed through its buffers. This one was captioned 'Running Over Target.'

The message was clear. The principles of effective project management may seem, to the uninitiated, a rather abstruse and perhaps pedantic set of disciplines. And yet, if we fail to apply these principles to managing change, the effects may be catastrophic. As we have seen in the previous chapter and elsewhere in this book, the first step to effective change is to kick the organisation into action – through clear goals, a sense of direction, an appropriate sequence of activity, and the energy and commitment to maintain momentum. These elements are essential to achieving change. Nevertheless, in most organisations this visible dynamism has also to be supported by a more mundane, but equally critical, commitment to detail – to systematic planning, to the allocating and monitoring of activity, and to the tracking of resources. In short, effective change requires effective project management. And, very often, it is this attention to the mechanics of change that ensures that the show is kept on the road during those inevitable phases when our vision becomes clouded or our energy wanes.

Planning the change

It is a truism that if we fail to plan, we plan to fail. In other words, if we embark on a significant change process without a clear idea not just of where we are going but also of how we are going to get there, the chances are that we shall run into difficulties sooner rather than later.

In general, the more effort we put into planning before starting the work, the fewer problems we shall face later.

Project-planning, though, is not simply about preparing highly detailed lists of tasks and activities. More importantly, in the early stages, it is about taking a step back and asking ourselves some very basic questions, such as:

- What are we trying to achieve?

- What will the planned changes look like, and how shall we know when we have succeeded?

- What are our timescales?

- Who will be affected by the changes, and who should be involved in the process?

- What are the factors that are likely to prevent us achieving our objectives (and what factors might be helpful)?

- How do we break our overall objectives down into workable steps or stages?

These basic questions, however they are formulated, lie at the heart of most formal project-planning methodologies. They are simple questions (although they may have highly complicated answers), but we are often tempted to disregard them in our haste to make change happen. Even experienced project managers can sometimes overlook the fundamentals as they become engrossed in the planning details; it is not unknown, for instance, for project managers to produce comprehensive activity plans that entirely fail to address the real issue. One company, in its overeagerness to meet a new business challenge, managed to produce a highly sophisticated plan for cascading new product training to all its staff before realising that no one had been asked to produce the original training materials!

More commonly, we simply find ourselves putting enormous energies into making the best of an imperfect situation because we have not put sufficient thought into clarifying our aims and approach at the start. We jump to the conclusion that major changes are needed and plan accordingly, when a little more forethought might have shown that we could have achieved similar effects with relatively minor interventions. Or we rush to start developing solutions before we are fully clear about the nature of the problem. As a result, we end up with change processes that are either unnecessary or, worse still, counter-productive.

Our starting-point, therefore, should be to ensure clarity about our objectives: what issues are we aiming to address, and what are our core objectives? If these questions are answered fully and clearly, the appropriate solutions will often begin to emerge by themselves. Moreover, clarity about our overall goals will be invaluable at those points – almost inevitable in any change process – when we start to run into difficulties or when confidence starts to wane. If we know clearly where we are going, then we are usually prepared to experiment with alternative routes. In the absence of clear goals, managers often find themselves locked into one track, even when it is clearly leading to a dead end.

This is an important point. Effective project-planning is not about creating massive, arthritic documents that are then followed mechanistically to the letter (even if some project managers persist in operating in this way). Most organisations are now so fast-moving that any change-planning, however systematic and detailed, can only be provisional. Good planning is often not about providing a step-by-step guide to the route, but rather about giving an overview of the terrain that highlights the destination and some key landmarks or milestones on the way. It provides the framework within which flexibility can be exercised.

Developing the plans

Once the objectives are clear, the detail of the plan can be developed. In practice, the overall project goals generally need to be broken down into a series of achievable steps, with a series of subobjectives and deadlines that can be identified. In clarifying these steps, a range of issues has to be considered, such as identifying:

- *key dependencies or critical paths.* These are steps that have to be completed before the overall project can progress. In the example cited earlier, for instance, it is clear that the cascade of product training could not begin until the training materials had been produced (although, of course, the cascade process could still be planned and developed in advance).

- *critical timescale or deadline issues.* It might, for example, be necessary to build in lead-times for production or development activities such as ensuring that all staff are trained before implementing a new operational process. If so, we would need to allow sufficient time for the training.

- *possible risks and contingencies at each stage.* If there are critical paths or dependencies, for example, it may be necessary to consider what happens if these are not achieved. Is an interim solution available? Is it possible to make more resource available to complete the task? Can the same results be achieved in another way? What effect will these actions have on the end result? While it will not be possible to plan for every possible contingency (and it would probably be a waste of time to try to do so), any *major* risks should be identified.

- *potential for parallel activity*. For most organisations today trying to manage change, time is a critical factor: it may be necessary to respond urgently to competitor or market pressures or to achieve rapid improvements in operational performance. In an ideal world, our planning might be largely sequential, with each step completed before we move on to the next. In practice, we shall often need to ensure that as many activities as possible are completed in parallel, so that we minimise the overall timescales of the project. This may mean accepting initial results that are less than perfect, aiming for further refinement as the project proceeds. It is important to distinguish the absolute critical paths (ie it is genuinely impossible to start Step 2 until Step 1 is complete) from those on which we can make a start even though some of the details or resources are not yet in place.

There is, of course, a variety of standard or proprietary tools that can be used to support this planning activity, including an increasing number of computer-based methodologies. The detail of these lies outside the scope of this book, but more detailed accounts of the mechanics of project management are recommended in the Further Reading section.

In practice, regardless of which tools are used, project-planning is rarely a neat activity, particularly in the context of dynamic change. It may be necessary to accept that some elements of the plan are unpredictable or that the plans for later stages may themselves be dependent on the outcomes of the initial phases. It is better to be honest about these uncertainties and simply to plan how they will be handled at the appropriate time, rather than formulate unrealistic plans that fall apart as soon as circumstances change. Indeed, in dealing with organisational change, it is often helpful to plan in discrete phases, with defined review and decision points at the end of each phase.

Planning resources

Once the key steps have been identified, it is possible to begin identifying the resources needed to deliver each step. The nature, mix and level of resources required will in turn help to determine the project structure and methodology. Resourcing elements may include:

- people

- finance

- equipment or technology

- accommodation

- specialist knowledge or expertise

- available timescales.

The identification of resources will often, in itself, begin to define the most appropriate shape and structure for the project. For example, if the change process requires a high level of specialist expertise, this may mean it is necessary to establish a highly specialised change team in order to plan and implement the activities. Alternatively, if the required expertise is not available in-house, this may mean that we need to employ external consultancy help to support the change process. Similarly, if the change process requires a high level of staffing against a relatively tight deadline, this may imply that a dedicated full-time team is required or, again, that external support is obtained.

Resource planning is generally a matter of balancing the overall project requirements against the various resource constraints that are present in all organisations in order to identify the most effective compromise. The key elements are shown in Figure 12:

Figure 12

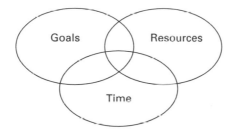

As Figure 12 suggests, in managing the change process our aim is generally to achieve a workable balance between the defined change objectives, the proposed timescales and the available resources. In an ideal world, we would have adequate internal resources to deliver the required project goals to the desired deadline. In practice, our goals will certainly be demanding, and may turn out to be overambitious. Our timescales will generally be short and be influenced by all kinds of external imperatives. And our resources are always finite and are rarely in the preferred form. We may, for example, have staff available, but without the required level of expertise. We may have the required equipment, but lack the staff to operate it. We may have funding available to resource the project, but still face major delays in recruiting the skills required. And these, of course, are the positive scenarios: in most organisations, there will be plenty of occasions when the required resources are simply lacking in any form.

In most cases, the starting-point is to identify how the available resource might be juggled in order to meet the requirement. Is it possible quickly to provide the available staff with the required skills, perhaps through an intensive training programme? Can we bring in external skills through a consultancy firm or a contractor? Can we move skilled staff around internally, perhaps through backfilling less critical areas with lower-skilled staff? And, in each case, what will be the financial or other business implications of these decisions?

Ultimately, we may decide that, however creative we are in developing these options, we still lack the resources required to deliver the project. If this is the case, we have no option but to address the other two elements shown in Figure 12. We may need to apply more realistic timescales or set less ambitious change objectives. In the context of project planning, these are perfectly reasonable choices (even if they may be difficult to sell in the organisation!). There is no point in applying unrealistic goals or deadlines if all the available evidence indicates that these are unachievable.

Too many change initiatives founder simply because the objectives are impracticable. We flounder on, trying to achieve the unachievable, until finally denial becomes impossible and we end up either admitting defeat or, perhaps more commonly, trying to cobble together some halfway acceptable solution from the resulting mess. Although failed project managers will construct highly detailed explanations of why they missed their objectives, it is worth remembering the equation:

No result × Detailed explanation of all the good reasons = No result

In other words, no amount of detailed explanation will change the fact that the desired outcome has not been delivered. If it appears, during the initial identification and planning phase, that the defined objectives are unrealistic, it is much better to be honest at that stage. There is still time then to amend the plans, through consultation with the key stakeholders of the proposed change. In this way, it is possible to ensure that, although the original change goals are compromised, the terms of the compromise reflect the priorities of all the parties involved. We may, for instance, decide that we can tolerate longer timescales or accept a phased approach that does not deliver all the required outcomes immediately. Conversely, we may decide that some of the original objectives, although desirable, were not essential. And, of course, there is always a chance that, if they are still wedded to the original goals and timescales, the organisational powers-that-be might accept the need to invest more resources.

In short, realism in planning is critical to the success of implementing change. This does not mean, however, that our planning should be unduly pessimistic. There has been growing evidence in recent years, particularly through the use of what is sometimes called 'breakthrough thinking', that organisations and the individuals within them are capable of delivering unexpectedly high levels of performance. If we set demanding goals, people often demonstrate extraordinary ingenuity in achieving them. If we shy away from setting the goals in the first place, then we shall never know what might have been achieved.

This takes us back to our starting-point in this chapter: clarity about our overall aims. In managing change, we should not be afraid to set and to work towards challenging objectives, but equally we should be prepared to question and challenge these as the planning and implementation proceed. If problems start to arise, therefore, we should review our project plans against our underpinning aims: what are we really trying to achieve here? As we get involved in the minutiae of the change process, it is often easy to confuse ends with means: organisations doggedly pursue their chosen strategy even when it is clearly not working and, in practice, the same or similar results might be achieved in other ways. Genuine 'breakthrough' achievements are, in most cases, likely to be delivered not through an intransigent pursuit of the impossible but through the creative consideration of all the possible means of achieving the desired goal. Similarly, Rosabeth Moss Kanter, in her book *The Change Masters*, argues that breakthrough changes, particularly in larger organisations, 'are more likely to represent the accumulation of accomplishments and tendencies built up slowly over time and implemented cautiously'.

The architecture of change

In part, as we have seen, the structure of the change process will be dictated by the available resource: for example, the balance between in-house staff and external support, or the balance between specialists and generalists. Apart from these practical considerations, however, other factors may well contribute to the overall architecture of the change process. These may include:

- actual or potential resistance to change

- 'political' considerations – eg the perceived authority or credibility of different areas of the organisation

- issues of integration or co-ordination across the organisation – eg the extent to which it is necessary to achieve consistent standards or practices

- diverse agendas among the change drivers or stakeholders

- the nature or structure of the organisation itself – eg the extent to which it is geographically diverse, or decentralised in its management or operational processes.

Each of these factors – many of which we discuss in more detail elsewhere – may potentially influence the kinds of methodology or 'architecture' required to implement change effectively. For instance, if there is likely to be significant resistance to the proposed changes, it may be appropriate to establish a change structure that provides additional reinforcement to the change objectives. Elements of this might include:

- ensuring visible senior-management commitment, perhaps through a steering group or equivalent. One organisation undertaking a major change initiative established a formal process of 'signing off' each step of the process at board level, primarily to provide demonstrable evidence of the senior team's commitment to the process.

- using high-profile or strongly credible external consultants to lead or facilitate the overall process. If the consultant leads the process, this may be seen as implying a lack of ownership by the organisation itself. However, many organisations feel that the support of an external facilitator provides additional 'objective' authority to the decisions and actions taken by the change team. This can be particularly useful if there are conflicting agendas in the organisation (including, perhaps, vested interests in the *status quo*) or if there is some perceived lack of credibility or authority among the change leaders

- creating a cross-functional or cross-divisional change team to ensure that there is an appropriate level of commitment from all the relevant stakeholder areas.

Similar kinds of structures can also be applied, in various permutations, to respond to the other factors listed above. For example, cross-functional change teams may provide a useful mechanism for dealing with the need to ensure consistent standards or to help manage change across a highly heterogeneous or geographically diverse organisation. When Royal Mail undertook a major reorganisation of its divisional structure a few years ago, it established a network of 'interlinking' change teams to manage the change process at both a divisional and functional level. Cross-functional teams planned and implemented the changes within each new division, working to agreed standard 'templates'. Each member of these teams then met with their functional colleagues on a national basis to ensure consistency of practice and standards. The whole network then reported, through a series of formalised channels, to an overarching steering group

With increasing globalisation and the widening use of communications technology, many organisations are now developing these kinds of structures on a 'virtual' basis – that is, establishing change teams that may be geographically diverse but that operate closely through technology. One of the increasing benefits of computer-based project management tools, for instance, is that they enable common project management disciplines to be applied, in 'real time', by team members who may have relatively little, if any, face-to-face contact. Project plans can be updated and communicated, progress can be monitored, and outcomes or issues can be reported. Alongside this, communications technology such as corporate intranets can provide all members with instant access to project materials, background data, common standards or policies, plans or illustrations, and all the various other items that traditionally might have been provided at project meetings. Using these kinds of technology, global businesses such as Texas Instruments are increasingly managing major change and development projects on a transnational basis.

The use of such 'virtual' teams to manage change carries countless implications, both positive and negative. On the positive side, it enables larger organisations to make best and most efficient use of the resources available to them, regardless of where those resources happen to be physically located. On the negative side, it brings a whole new set of management challenges. Managers who are leading or participating in virtual teams have commented on the difficulty of, for example, managing performance or delivery when traditional face-to-face interactions are missing.

In general, the management process is likely to become much more formalised, with the emphasis on measurable outputs, but many of the usual 'cues' or early warnings about problems will be missing. The traditional 'hands-on' change manager will become skilled in recognising potential issues – anxieties about targets, failure to deal with problems, lack of initiatives, and so on – before they become serious. In the virtual team, these may often be disguised behind formal documentation, so that problems are not evident until they begin to affect results. Equally, the team member has no opportunity to raise issues informally or casually, which may mean that potential concerns are held back until they become significant.

All of this implies that, in managing the virtual change team, we need both to impose relatively rigorous management monitoring and control and to identify and promote opportunities for less formal interaction. It is important actually to bring the team together on a periodic basis during the life of the project, if possible, and to make good day-to-day use of less structured communications media, such as electronic mail or teleconferencing. Contrary to some business practice, there may also be benefits in supporting, rather than discouraging, communication that is not directly related to the project itself. If participants begin to build up informal relationships through the use of, say, electronic mail (e-mail), this may well provide opportunities for them to discuss relevant issues in a less formal context.

Individual contribution

So far in this chapter we have talked about the mobilisation and management of collective resources to ensure that change is delivered. In the end, though, effective change usually depends on a series of individual contributions and actions that needs to be co-ordinated and managed. Elsewhere in the book, we discuss issues of power in managing change, and how organisational power and authority can be harnessed to ensure change delivery.

Ironically, however, the project manager responsible for delivering change often has relatively little power in the conventional sense. For all the reasons we have described above, change teams are often cross-functional and frequently part-time. Members are commonly charged with delivering change, while also ensuring that they continue to achieve day-to-day operational targets. In this context, even when there is high-level commitment to the change process, change leaders often find themselves coming lower in the pecking order than their functional colleagues. The team members' priority may well be to their 'home' function, and, when push comes to shove, it may well be that delivering this period's targets is given a higher priority than achieving a long-term change goal. These problems can be addressed, of course, by techniques that we explore in other chapters. Nevertheless, the change manager's role is often less about giving and enforcing instructions than about promoting and managing commitment to mutually agreed objectives. There are a number of keys to this:

- first, ensuring that all parties fully buy in to the change objectives. If team members harbour doubts or reservations at the early stages, these will undermine commitment, and therefore performance, as the project progresses. There is generally benefit in holding an initial workshop session both to help build the sense of a team and to enable members to explore their views about the change objectives. Clearly, in the context of virtual teams this is likely to be even more critical.

- second, agreeing as precisely as possible the tasks and objectives of each member of the team during each phase of the project. Although it is clearly essential that these are in line with the overall goals of the change project, it is also important that they are genuinely agreed with the individual concerned, rather than simply imposed. If the individual has reservations about his or her ability to deliver the objectives, for whatever reasons, it is better that these are raised and explored at the start of the process. It is also critical that these agreed goals are not left woolly or ill-defined, but are in line with SMART criteria – that is, as well as being Agreed, they should be Specific, Measurable, Realistic and Time-Bound. We can then track, meaningfully, whether they are being delivered.

- third, and perhaps most important, the process of project management should aim to be an exercise in collective problem-solving rather than an apportioning of blame. Unless you are extremely fortunate, the project will go off track at various points – that, after all, is why project managers are needed. When this happens, it is tempting to begin berating individuals for having failed to deliver. In practice, though, except in extreme cases, there will generally be good reasons why problems have arisen – changes in circumstances, unforeseen barriers, unexpected complications. There is usually little point in worrying about whose fault it is. The most constructive approach is to accept the situation, and then – working as a team, if possible – begin to identify ways in which you might help the individual pull things back on track, perhaps through more resources or a different approach, or by accepting a compromise outcome.

As we indicated at the start of this chapter, in today's dynamic organisational environment change cannot be implemented through a rigid, one-dimensional approach to project management. Rather, we need to balance clear objectives with flexibility in action and decision-making. Through the above techniques, change implementation can become a matter of mutual support, with individual team members committed both to the aims of the project and to each other. They will be reluctant to let their colleagues down by failing to deliver but, equally, they will be willing to raise their concerns or problems at an early stage, confident that they will receive appropriate support and assistance. With this kind of culture in place, the role of the change manager becomes much easier, and the success of the change process becomes much more assured.

GUIDELINES

- *Take* a step back in the early stages of planning change and ask some basic questions in order to ensure full understanding of your aims, targets and timescales.

- *Don't aim*, in planning change, for a step-by-step guide to the route, but for an overview highlighting your main goals and some key landmarks or milestones on the way – that is, a framework within which flexibility can be exercised.

- *Break* down overall project goals into a series of achievable steps, with subobjectives and deadlines as appropriate. Identify critical paths, risks, timescales and opportunities for parallel activity.

- *Accept* that some elements of the project will be unpredictable, and that plans for later stages may be dependent on the outcomes of the initial phases.

- *Aim* for a workable balance between the defined change objectives, the proposed timescales and the available resources.

- *Try* to establish, if there is likely to be significant resistance to the proposed changes, a change structure that provides additional reinforcement to the change objectives – for example, through senior management commitment, use of external consultants, or the creation of cross-functional teams.

- *Apply*, in managing 'virtual' change teams, relatively rigorous management controls, while also promoting opportunities for informal interaction.

- *Ensure* clear individual commitment and accountability from all those involved in delivering the change objectives. Focus on defining clear objectives, and aim to manage individual performance through constructive discussion rather than criticism or blame.

11　Experimenting

Groucho Marx took one of his brothers to an expensive country golf resort. Claiming to be a golf wizard, the brother hit the first ball, smashing a car windscreen. The second broke a resort window. Groucho exited rapidly, without his funny walk.

Like Groucho's brother, anyone who has used a golf club soon discovers that this particular device can have unpredictable results. Much the same discovery can be made in organisations – there are relatively few reliable levers of change. As with selecting a golf club, whatever change lever you choose is a matter of judgement and often you must be willing to accept unpredictable results.

Managers are surrounded by uncertainty and trends, such as those outlined in Chapter 1 on Models, including:

- exchange rates

- cost of energy

- outcome of mergers, demergers

- foreign competition

- technology

- consumer tastes.

Not every aspect of a particular change effort will be unpredictable. For instance, it may be quite possible to anticipate that what you want to achieve will meet resistance. Or that the decision to cut your product price will produce a definite response from your competitors. Because making changes means living with a certain amount of uncertainty, this is sometimes used unjustifiably as an excuse for avoiding or delaying action.

The fact that the outcome from a particular change is uncertain is seldom an argument for doing absolutely nothing. It warrants a review of the scenarios that might arise if change is implemented. Managerial leaders recognise that in many respects planned change is unpredictable. They therefore:

- *review* the different types of change actions available

- *consider* what aspects of the change can be predicted – what the likely scenarios are

- *track* the results of a change effort

- *respond* quickly and flexibly to new and unpredicted events.

If you manage a number of subordinates, try to convey to them that their efforts to make things happen are supported, as long as reasonable efforts have been made to think about the likely consequences. For small-scale change efforts, minimise the demand for documentation. Large-scale change should always be documented in advance, as this provides a way of taking a critical look at what is proposed and a baseline from which to judge how well or badly the change effort goes.

Both the unpredictable nature and the scale of change that you may be seeking must figure in your thinking. Figure 13 summarises the situation.

Figure 13

Effects and outcomes

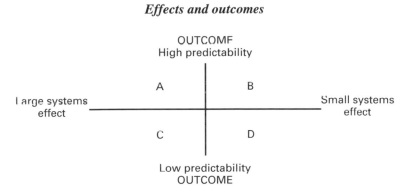

To achieve a major change you would normally prefer your selected change actions to be in sector A, where the outcome is highly predictable. In reality, however, you may have to be reconciled to a high degree of uncertainty, as in sector C. Even if you want a relatively small change, the outcome may still tally with sector D, ie be hard to predict, because you cannot be sure that the particular change lever will perform as expected. The search for certainty, or minimised uncertainty, is often a critical factor in deciding whether a particular change effort will succeed.

A particular change action may work for you, yet fail dismally when tried by subordinates. For example, some managers love sending ticklers or 'reminders' that they are expecting some job to be done by a certain date. If this is part of their style, it can produce results. Other managers, however, find that this approach does not seem effective when they try it, and they have to resort to phone calls or personal visits to make something happen. Similarly, some managers bent on major strategic change may rely heavily on market research or structural rearrangements, while others find that for them these are too slow and ineffective.

Experiments

Peer into a car mechanic's tool box and you will usually see dozens of different-sized spanners. Watch the mechanic choose one. Often the first tool selected does not fit, and it is only by trial and error that the right one is located.

Like the mechanic, managers who want to make things happen must be prepared to experiment until they find the right lever of change that produces results. Working by trial and error (now sometimes called an iterative approach) is a relatively new approach for some organisations. The myth still exists that managers must always get it right first time and that organisations, particularly public bodies, cannot afford any mistakes.

Management science, with its emphasis on quantifying and rationality, has come to be regarded as almost a panacea for making organisations successful. Experiments on a large scale are therefore often condemned as irresponsible, too costly or a sign that not enough original research has been done to minimise uncertainty.

The man epitomising this scientific approach to management was Robert MacNamara who, with his colleagues, invaded the beleaguered Ford car corporation just after World War II. The Whizz Kids, as they were called, arrived as a package, selling themselves as a complete team to the company. They brought with them extraordinary skills of numeracy. Delving into every part of the crumbling car giant, they asked endless questions. For a while they were dismissed as the Quiz kids.

The kids measured just about everything, and the power of their information overwhelmed their critics. Their success in transforming Ford influenced several generations of managers, though the price has been high. Numbers and analysis have since dominated management thinking, particularly in some of the major international corporations, and the scope for experimentation has been drastically curtailed and sometimes virtually destroyed.

Gradually, managers around the world have begun to realise that quantifying, analysis and rationality have a built-in conservative bias that values certainty above creativity and stifles change by tolerating only minimal experimentation. Aiming at near certainty frequently means banishing experiments and, ultimately, success.

A serious criticism of business schools has been that their graduates rely on the analytical approach, focusing mainly on short-term goals, with little recognition of the value of vision and long-term investment. This kind of excessive rationality, which has characterised much of management thinking, has even infected organisations immune to the products of business schools. In Japan, for instance, a passion for numbers, order and quantifying has occasionally proved obstructive. For years, the giant Nissan car firm was run by numbers-oriented finance experts who fiercely resisted the anguished pleas of committed employees, based in the USA, to experiment with models adapted for the US market.

All the values of our culture seem to favour routine over creativity, the well-established over novelty, the comfortable over the uncomfortable, boredom over excitement and precision over approximation. Managers are paid to be right, and career prospects depend on avoiding mistakes. It is hardly surprising that experimentation and hence new products often stem from outside the industries and organisations that, logically, ought to be producing them.

Consumer-product companies, for example, will often have a department or a specialist post devoted to new products. Because few managers want to put their name to a failure, the result is endless idea generation, concept development, concept-testing, market research and so on. But the new products never seem to reach the market. One top marketing expert asks his clients who are looking for a new product, 'How much are you prepared to lose?' If they cannot carry the loss of failure, he argues, they cannot afford to go ahead with it.

Even failed experiments can teach something, so that the next attempts have a greater chance of success. Unfortunately, finance-oriented directors and senior managers seldom see it that way. They are usually intolerant of failure, always demanding proof that success is a near certainty.

Because so many organisations suffer from an inability to handle experiments, there has been a search for ways to make them possible, despite the obstacles and organisational inertia. The most radical way has been the advent of the transforming leader who shakes the organisation from top to bottom, revitalising it with new vision and the courage to experiment (see Chapter 2 on Leadership).

Rather less grandiose, yet in some ways just as radical, is the idea of the product champion, who pushes for a particular development within an organisation. This person is expected to thrust past organisational constraints and be willing to experiment. Product champions generally identify themselves; the problem for organisations is how to help them succeed. A product champion will often try numerous new ways to bring about change in the search for something that works. This experimental learning approach makes them highly vulnerable:

- Look what he's cost us!

- His idea was crazy anyway.

- She should never have been allowed to try it.

- Who needs failures?

- I knew that it wouldn't work.

Of the many lessons to learn about using product champions to foster experimentation and hence change, probably the most important is:

Don't let a product champion go down with the product or idea.

Product champions who have put their careers on the line in order to experiment with change must be rewarded, not punished, and recognised, not given the cold shoulder. Less radical, yet still highly effective, is the approach epitomised by the 3M company 'to make a little, sell a little, make a little more' – in other words, being willing to create a host of experiments and, if they show signs of succeeding, to back them further.

Having dozens of experiments happening simultaneously has several obvious advantages. First, the chances of a winning idea is increased simply by the law of averages. Secondly, by having so many experiments at once, it is harder for those who resist change to block them all. Some slip through unopposed or with only token resistance.

Studies of highly successful companies show that major change often arises from one or more people sneaking off and experimenting, often without official sanction. In the case of new products this may mean using scrounged materials, working overtime and relying on the goodwill from colleagues. Meanwhile the megabucks are being spent elsewhere. Time and again these major plans hit obstacles or lose credibility until, like the Fifth Cavalry, the more modest experiments pop up to save the day.

Thus, an important contribution to promoting change is assisting these low-level, often unofficial experiments. If you cannot actively fund them, then at least turn a blind eye to people doing them. Whether the experiments concern people, products or cash, the results are unpredictable. Failure is always possible. Too often organisations have a culture of punishment for failed experiments. Punishment may be reflected in damage to one's career or some other unpleasant response, such as criticism or disciplinary action. Rules, procedures and tight controls tend to be developed as managers legislate against experiments that might fail. In these circumstances, only the brave or the foolhardy stick their necks out and attempt new ways of achieving better results.

Long-term strategic change cannot flourish in a culture that punishes failed experiments, and this is why few really new organisational thrusts occur. Gradually, the organisation becomes rigid and slow in its responses, unable to take advantage of new opportunities.

The language of experimentation is easy to recognise. People can be heard saying things like:

- Let's try it!

- Why don't we test it out?

- What will happen if . . .?

- If we did that, how would we know whether it succeeds or fails?

- If it doesn't work, we'll try something else.

- Here's one way of finding out.

- What do our customers think?

- We tried it and found. . . .

Equally, you can tell when the climate is unfavourable to strategic change. People say things like:

- Too risky.

- It could go really wrong.

- We can't afford to learn by trial and error.

- What counts is success.

- You'd better be right.

- You're ignoring the procedures.

- Go ahead but, if it goes wrong, you're on your own.

- If we do that, we'll tip off the opposition.

The last of these is a familiar catechism of some companies who reject experiments in the marketplace because they fear that this will alert their competitors. In practice, the failure to experiment is a worse fault, cutting them off from customers and learning how to meet market needs. What drives many experiments forward is the customer. Getting close to the customer often provides a vital force for trying something new.

GUIDELINES

- *Consider* what results of planned change can be broadly predicted – what are the likely scenarios?

- *Experiment* with different change actions till you get results.

- *Avoid* the paralysis of analysis.

- *Pay attention* to organisational values and culture – this will encourage an experimental approach.

- *Minimise* documentation for small-scale change efforts.

- *Favour* creativity over routine.

- *Welcome* the failed experiment as a chance to learn.

- *Don't let* a product champion go down with the product or idea.

- *Try out* lots of ideas. Sheer quantity will often produce a winner.

- *Listen* for and speak the language of experimentation.

- *Get* closer to the customer to generate more experiments.

12 Participative decision-making

The Employment Service, like the majority of the semi-autonomous agencies created from the Civil Service, has undergone dramatic structural and cultural change over the last decade. Agency status was intended to introduce new operational freedoms in delivering Government policy and so produce significant improvements in the quality and efficiency of service provision.

In turn, though, this new status has brought major challenges for managers and staff working in the organisation, many of whom were highly sceptical about the organisation's capacity to change. In responding to these challenges, one region – building on a series of previous change initiatives – decided to implement a radical approach. To build commitment to the change process managers organised a series of planning events for large groups of employees – up to 600 staff at the largest event – with the explicit intention of involving the widest possible constituency of experience and opinion.

The sessions were carefully designed by a team that itself reflected the diversity of the staff who would be attending the event, and all participants were expected to contribute to the resulting plans and decisions. The events have addressed a wide range of issues including, at national level, the development of corporate goals and values.

At first glance, this approach contradicts the received wisdom that planning is best handled by individuals or small groups. In practice, and through careful management, these large-scale events have proved remarkably successful not only in promoting shared understanding across the organisation but also in ensuring maximum commitment to the resulting change.

Changing the *status quo* usually requires support. Participation can help to obtain that support. United Technology, an American high-tech company based in New England, once defined the aim of a programme to promote participative management as 'empowering others and gaining support in the organisation'.

International studies show that the more participatory the firm, the greater its financial and other types of success. This is especially so when introducing new technology. What happened when New Scotland Yard, the London police headquarters, installed a huge

Command and Control Complex is an example of linking technology decisions with participation.

The Complex changed jobs and working practices for both uniformed and civilian staff. Sophisticated equipment had to be installed and old skills replaced by new ones. An authoritarian approach to such a major change would have backfired, leading to inefficiency and low morale.

Staff from many departments and all levels joined teams to find solutions to a mass of problems. These ranged from the design and lay-out of the equipment and where it was to be installed, to the best type of chair for seating comfortably a 6-foot, 16-stone policeman or a rather lighter 5-foot-4-inch policewoman.

Care was taken to involve staff fully in decision-making. The team leading the changes marked the dimensions of the real location at New Scotland Yard on the floor of an empty warehouse. Templates and mock-ups were moved about into different shapes, then tested for suitability. Criticism and suggestions were encouraged with a free interchange of ideas and comments. Where possible, the team searched for consensus.

The result is a smooth-running complex in which police and civilians enjoy a quiet, unstressed atmosphere, each operator working efficiently. Participation has clearly paid off. According to the UK government's Work Research Unit, greater involvement of employees in managing change and decisions helps organisations become more:

- *profitable* – through improved quality and lower unit costs

- *able* to use their human resources

- *robust*

- *adaptable*

- *viable* in the long term

- *creative*

- *effective* and quicker at making changes.

When employees are involved, better decisions are reached and with more commitment to making them work.

Nailing down participation

Participation occurs when people are involved and influence decisions that are likely to affect them. At one extreme, zero participation means that employees do as they are told. At the other extreme, total delegated authority ensures that employees have the final say. Participation happens only between these extremes. It does not happen when there is either total management control or total worker control.

Participative decision-making expands the influence in the organisation of those who are lower down the hierarchy and affected by decisions. The two routes for achieving this are via:

* *industrial democracy* – collective bargaining, through representatives

* *participative management* – informal sharing of decision-making at the workplace, involving individuals.

The most widespread form of participation is the formal process by which employers and trade unions negotiate agreements. Highly structured and frequently bureaucratic, it often raises false expectations about the extent to which employees will be involved. A disillusioned employers' association in Sweden called it 'a gigantic apparatus for the creation of dissatisfaction'. Despite this, industrial democracy can lead to useful involvement in decisions and joint problem-solving.

Participative management is an informal process. It relies on affecting people's behaviour not through constitutions but by managers talking directly with those who will be affected by the decisions. The two approaches thus take a different view on who will be involved. Formal systems focus on representatives, informal ones on individuals. Hence participation methods differ, as follows:

Individual	Representative
Briefing groups	Collective bargaining
Attitude surveys	Joint consultation
Problem-solving groups	Works councils
Job enrichment	Worker directors
Autonomous work groups	Staff committees

These two approaches are not mutually exclusive, however. Participative decision-making usually fails when managers rely on only one of the two approaches. Both are needed if the pattern of organisational decision-making is going to be successfully altered.

Exclusive reliance on one or other approach leads employees to see participative decision-making as manipulative and a ploy to remove resistance.

The ingredients

The above clarifies what we mean by participative decision-making and some of its benefits. There are also several important ingredients to participative decision-making, such as:

- individual autonomy

- group responsibility

- organisation-wide influence

- the nature of the decision-making process.

Individual autonomy
Enhancing individual autonomy in organisations is increasingly recognised as a key to obtaining employee commitment to change. The Computer Management Group, for instance, which operates in the UK, the Netherlands and Germany with a staff of more than 1,000, has a written philosophy that begins:

> CMG is a successful company where each person is his or her own boss to the maximum possible extent.

Once people have achieved some of the more basic survival requirements in life, they seek opportunities for self-expression, satisfaction in what they do and an ability to arrange their own worklives as far as possible.

Giving people more autonomy or control over their lives does not lead to anarchy: it fosters responsibility and accountability. These make it easier to confront change, promote innovation and tackle inertia.

Group responsibility
Individual employees are usually part of a team or local work group. The latter is part of a larger group, department, division, subsidiary and so on. Both individuals and groups have a responsibility to the organisation.

Sometimes the groups' needs override those of individuals, and occasionally *vice versa*. Participative decision-making recognises this fact by encouraging groups to take responsibility for their own actions. Individuals must exercise autonomy both within and outside the group. Participative decision-making provides a spur to groups becoming committed to change.

Organisation-wide influence
Once you start trusting people to take part in the decision-making process the effect is like a stone dropped into a pool of water, with ripples spreading throughout the enterprise.

Managers in both UT and New Scotland Yard obtained better results by letting many people have a direct influence on the decision-making process. They realised that when both individuals and groups exercise their autonomy, the benefits extend across the organisation.

The decision process
The decision-making process is shown in Figure 14. Several thousand managers and supervisors have confirmed that the nine-step process reflects what happens when organisations make choices.

If you want to promote participative decision-making, there are three useful check questions that can be applied anywhere along the paths shown in the chart:

- *type* – what sort of decision is open to participation?

- *stages* – where in the decision-making process will participation occur?

- *extent* – how far will participation go, and who will be involved?

Type

Not every decision is suitable for participation. For instance, if you are introducing short-time working, redundancy and closure, it will almost certainly fail.

Even if everyone is fully committed, the scope for participation varies according to the type of decision, as shown in Box 21. The management task is creatively to seek ways to expand opportunities for participation, where appropriate.

Stages

The nine-stage process shown in Figure 14 is a useful aid for clarifying

Figure 14

The nine-phase decision-making process

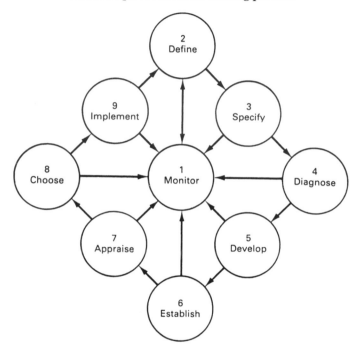

1 *Monitor* the environment constantly.

2 *Define* the decision-problem or situation. In other words, state precisely the boundaries.

3 *Specify* the decision objectives. Clarify what you expect to achieve; define the risks and constraints.

4 *Diagnose* the problem or situation and analyse causes.

5 *Develop* alternative courses of action or solutions.

6 *Establish* the methodology or criteria for appraising alternatives.

7 *Appraise* alternative solutions or courses of action.

8 *Choose* the best alternative solution or course of action.

9 *Implement* the best alternative solution or course of action.

Source: 'How to make a business decision, an analysis of theory and practice', Archer ER. *Management Review*, February 1980, p58. Printed with the permission of the publisher, copyright 1980 by A Macom, a division of American Management Associations. All rights reserved.

where participation will be possible and managerially acceptable. Although the eighth stage of selecting alternatives is perhaps the most important, it is often mistaken for the entire decision process. Uncertainty about where participation is desirable may cause decision-making to become diffuse – a slow, creeping consensus. This happened during the early 1980s when the Philips electrical group relied heavily on achieving participation and consensus in the eighth choice stage. This not only maintained the *status quo* but also prevented responsibility from being clearly located. A major shake-up in the second half of the decade shifted the balance towards participation in the other stages, key managers taking responsibility for final choices.

Box 21

Decision bands	
Decision band	*Scope*
BAND E	Policy making
BAND D	Programming – broad planning of execution of policy
BAND C	Interpretive – specific action decisions from range of options
BAND B	Routine – choice of how to do what is already specified
BAND A	Automatic – choice of operations within set process
BAND O	Vegetative – minimal discretion

Extent

How much participation will there be? Although it can occur in any of the nine decision stages, the extent may vary, as shown in Box 22. Participation does not mean that everybody makes the decision or that there must always be consensus. For instance, a chemical firm that was highly committed to participative decision-making involved all its employees in considering how it should spend £2 million on further research. Many people shared in analysing opportunities, developing different courses of action, appraising alternatives and so on. Everyone was also aware that the ultimate choice of a course of action – the actual decision point – was reserved for the board of directors.

Similarly, in developing its participative management style the Formica Company, a leading producer of decorative laminates, identified these constraints:

No loss of control of strategic decisions at senior management level

No reduction in individual responsibility as a result of participation.

Box 22

		Participation process gauge	
A	Management makes a decision without any discussion with employees. Employees are not informed of the decision afterwards.	ZERO
B	Management makes a decision without any prior discussion with employees, and simply informs them of it afterwards.	INFORMATION (one-way)
C	Management makes a decision without prior discussion with employees, and afterwards informs them of it and explains the reasons behind the decisions.	INFORMATION bordering on COMMUNICATION (two-way)
D	Management sorts out its ideas, makes a plan, asks employees for their views, but tells them that because of other constraints their views can make little or no difference to the decision itself.	COMMUNICATION bordering on CONSULTATION
E	Management sorts out its ideas, makes a plan, asks employees for their views, and fully takes them into account in making the final decision.	CONSULTATION
F	Management fully shares the problem with employees without any preconceived plan – but after all the talking management makes the decision.	CONSULTATION bordering on DECISION BY AGREEMENT
G	Management fully shares the problem without any preconceived plan – and after all the talking, a decision is agreed.	DECISION BY AGREEMENT
H	Management identifies the problem and asks employees to find and implement a solution.	DELEGATED AUTHORITY

Source: Adapted from *Industrial Participation* by D Wallace Bell, London, Pitman, 1979

Participation appears to have the effect of increasing the control exercised by employees without decreasing that of managers. In more participative companies, managers generally report feeling that they exercise more influence than managers in less participative companies. This is not only reassuring but also points to another myth about participation, namely that power is a fixed quantity – if someone gains it then someone else must lose it. The reality is that everyone's power can be increased by effective participative decision-making (see also Chapter 6 on Power and Influence).

Real participation does not eliminate control: it only changes its quality.

Who wants it?

Do employees actually want to participate? In decisions about their own immediate work situation, the answer is certainly yes. In middle and top management decisions, the answer is less sure, varying in different organisational and national cultures.

Employees are modest in their expectations. They are more likely to care about issues that impinge on their daily lives than they are about more distant topics such as how profits are distributed, whether the organisation should invest in bio-engineering and so on.

Lack of enthusiasm to participate in higher-level decisions may be due, though, to an unhelpful participation process. For instance, employees may conclude that on some issues they lack expertise. Unless the gap between subordinates and superiors is reduced, attempts at participation merely increase mistrust. Participation schemes that have been imposed (whether by politicians, trade union leaders or management) without being designed to meet the particular needs of the workforce are destined to failure.

A requisite of any system is that those involved should themselves have a say in the 'why', 'what', 'when' and 'how' of the system that is seen to be good for them. There should be a slow building of the awareness of shared goals, not an assumption that participation will automatically create a sense of common interest.

A decision aid

Of the various decision steps described in Figure 14 perhaps the most crucial is selecting the best alternative solution or course of action. Participation in this vital stage is seldom shared with more than a dozen people, and often far fewer.

A practical and enjoyable way of clarifying what must be decided and how much participation will be encouraged is now possible using a personal computer. The Priority Decision System (PDS), for example, was developed at Brunel University and has operated in actual work situations for several years. It can be used by a single manager or a whole team, and potentially involve many people in situations where choices must be made.

Organisations such as ICI, British Telecom, Essex County Council, IBM, Kodak, Lucas Aerospace, Shell and even the Cabinet Office have all used PDS. You need no knowledge of computers, because everything is presented in straightforward English with clear instructions.

The first step in using PDS is to list the choices being considered. For example, a management team that has to decide what projects to fund in the new financial year simply lists these in any order it chooses.

Next, you name the people who will be involved in making the actual decision. Some of these will have much less authority or power than others. Participative decision-making often fails because this uncertainty is never resolved.

PDS uses various methods to help decide how much influence each decision-maker will be given. We can see it working in practice in a notional company headed by managing director Brian Smith. The board, consisting of the MD and four other directors, has to make a decision about which of seven possible projects it will back for further development.

The example in Box 23 shows the results of the board's using PDS. The MD has emerged with more influence than any other single member of the board (26 per cent) yet without having more influence than his combined colleagues.

Box 23

Influence of decision-makers (using the Priority Decision System)		
PROBLEM NAME:	DM	
CRITERION USED:	ALL THINGS CONSIDERED	
METHOD USED:	SCALING	
RANK	**DECISION-MAKER**	**INFLUENCE**
1	A) MD: Brian Smith	0.261 (26.1%)
2	B) Director: P Jones	0.217 (21.7%)
2	D) Director: M White	0.217 (21.7%)
3	C) Director: L Brown	0.174 (17.4%)
4	E) Director: H Black	0.130 (13.0%)
	ALL DECISION-MAKERS	1.000 (100.0%)

The benefits of this approach are considerable. For instance, if MD Smith asserts that he is merely 'first among equals', he would have to demonstrate this by being allocated an equal weight among all the other decision-makers. Alternatively, as the most senior member of the team, he may expect to have more authority over a particular decision than his colleagues. Yet will his influence be sufficient to overrule everyone else? If so, what is the point of pretending that the members are participating? They are merely being consulted.

The results of the use of PDS by two of the board members are shown in Box 24. Directors White and Black do not entirely agree on how the projects should be ranked. Both selected Project 1 as the most important, giving different rankings to the others. When all the board members have used PDS, their views are combined to produce a team result, as shown in Box 25. Project 1 emerges as a winner. Even allowing for the differences between the individual members of the board, the computer system finds a high degree of agreement about the rankings.

Box 24

How two members of the Board rated the seven projects		
PROBLEM NAME: DM		
CRITERION USED: ALL THINGS CONSIDERED		
METHOD USED: MAGNITUDE ESTIMATION		
DECISION-MAKER: D) Director: M White		

RANK	OPTION	PRIORITY
1	A) PROJECT 1	0.180 (18.0%)
1	D) PROJECT 4	0.180 (18.0%)
2	C) PROJECT 3	0.157 (15.7%)
2	G) PROJECT 7	0.157 (15.7%)
3	E) PROJECT 5	0.135 (13.5%)
4	F) PROJECT 6	0.112 (11.2%)
5	B) PROJECT 2	0.079 (7.9%)
	ALL OPTIONS	1.000 (100.0%)

PROBLEM NAME: DM		
CRITERION USED: ALL THINGS CONSIDERED		
METHOD USED: MAGNITUDE ESTIMATION		
DECISION-MAKER: E) Director: H Black		

RANK	OPTION	PRIORITY
1	A) PROJECT 1	0.208 (20.8%)
2	C) PROJECT 3	0.182 (18.2%)
3	F) PROJECT 6	0.156 (15.6%)
3	D) PROJECT 4	0.156 (15.6%)
4	E) PROJECT 5	0.130 (13.0%)
5	B) PROJECT 2	0.091 (9.1%)
6	G) PROJECT 7	0.078 (7.8%)
	ALL OPTIONS	1.000 (100.0%)

Box 25

How the board ranked the projects

PROBLEM NAME: DM
CRITERION USED: ALL THINGS CONSIDERED
METHOD USED: MAGNITUDE ESTIMATION
DECISION-MAKER: TEAM

RANK	OPTION	PRIORITY
1	A) PROJECT 1	0.241 (24.1%)
2	C) PROJECT 3	0.181 (18.1%)
3	D) PROJECT 4	0.155 (15.5%)
4	B) PROJECT 2	0.125 (12.5%)
5	E) PROJECT 5	0.122 (12.2%)
6	F) PROJECT 6	0.089 (8.9%)
7	G) PROJECT 7	0.086 (8.6%)
ALL OPTIONS		1.000 (100.0%)

AGREEMENT MEASURE: 924
DECISION STANDARD: High degree of agreement between the team members

Seems complicated? Only in describing it. In practice the system rapidly reports on the decision-making. What takes the time is collecting the information and feeding it into the computer. Even this can be shortened by letting people type in their choices.

Any number of people can participate in PDS, although if the numbers exceed 20 it is necessary to do the decision-making in batches.

With greater clarity about who is taking part in the decision and their degree of influence, there is usually greater acceptance of the final result. There is less argument about why a particular course of action has been chosen and more sense of 'ownership' about the final decision. Maurice Hawker, a local government director in Essex, is blunt about the advantages: 'in place of watery compromises from four meetings, we get a valid consensus in 40 minutes'.

IPA

In the UK you can obtain help and advice about participative decision-making from the Industrial Participation Association (IPA). This is an independent, voluntary grouping of individuals and organisations spread across most sectors of industry, commerce, public corporations, educational bodies and so on.

GUIDELINES

- *Determine* people's expectations about and desire for participation.

- *Start* small. People need to get used to participative decision-making.

- *Avoid* top-heavy consultative structures.

- *Use* both formal and informal approaches to participation.

- *Decide* whether to link implementation of participation with pressing problems being experienced by the organisation.

- *Clarify* the issues for which participation is needed.

- *Identify* who is likely to be affected by a decision.

- *Ensure* that all parties with power participate.

- *Explain* where in the decision process participation will be permitted.

- *Distinguish* between consulting and participation.

- *Communicate* what is non-negotiable, where participation will not occur.

- *Create* a credible timetable in which participation can occur.

- *Convey* how people can participate – the mechanisms.

- *Help* people understand complex issues.

- *Enhance* individual autonomy to gain employee commitment to change.

- *Provide* feedback on how the input from participation has been used.

- *Model* a participative style, don't just exhort.

- *Look* for system-wide effects of participative decision-making.

- *Allocate* sufficient resources for the scheme including training and follow-up.

- *Assume* that participation will take a long time to become totally effective.

13   Outside agents

'What's the time?'
'Lend me your watch and I'll tell you!'

This quip can be related to the way many people see the work of outside consultants: they get paid to tell you what you already know. A more cynical opinion is that they only report convenient truths rather than uncomfortable facts. How else can they operate if they are to stay in business? Messengers bringing unpleasant news are seldom invited back. In direct contrast to the idea that consultants are useless is the belief that major organisational change is dependent on a master blueprint, best created with the help of an omniscient consultant or change agent.

It is certainly right to be sceptical of what outside change agents can offer. Why use them when the same results can often be achieved by people already in the company? Senior managers commonly underrate the skills that exist in-house.

However, outsiders can be especially useful in identifying and tackling situations that are spiralling downward:

Figure 15

Low performance and expectations

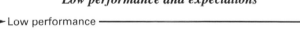

Having identified this situation, an outside agent attempts to turn it into one based on high expectations and high performance. Some of the problems of using outsiders and the advantages of using insiders are shown in Box 26. There may be particular benefits in having outsiders

157

work with a selected group of internal change agents. In the Metal Box company, for example, attaching some internal staff to work with consultants produced these benefits:

- reduced fee or shorter timescale

- less disruption to operations, because seconded staff were able to spot potential problems early

- a resource of people able to understand the consultant's work and thus able to trouble-shoot after the consultant has left

- a pool of people able to apply similar techniques to other issues.

Box 26

Using inside or outside change agents

Disadvantages of an outside change agent	*Advantages of an inside change agent*
Is a stranger	Knows the system, where power
May not identify with the	lies, and opinion leaders, and
problems	the strategic leverage points
Takes time fully to understand	Speaks the organisation's
values, culture and way	language – the special way
organisation works	members refer to things, the tone
May create dependency	and style of discussing things
Can generate resistance	Understands the norms and
Cost	commonly held beliefs,
Adverse impact on morale,	attitudes and behaviours
indicating lack of management	
confidence in existing staff	

Types of change agent

Anyone who alters the *status quo* within an organisation is a change agent. A consultant who is hired to do a particular piece of work on a fixed contract and then leaves once the work is completed is the simplest type of change agent. On the other hand, some consultants have permanent contracts, becoming virtually part of the organisation's staff, perhaps on a part-time basis. British Airways, for instance, brought in a number of outside consultants to supplement internal consulting staff for several years to assist in a massive staff development programme. Equally, an outside change agent could be someone from one part of the organisation intervening in a different part to alter the *status quo*.

Outside change agents broadly fall into two categories: those concerned with process, and those offering a techniques package. Those concerned with process study what is happening, with no set solution in mind. An example would be an organisational development specialist diagnosing a situation to enable managers to implement their own solutions.

Those offering a 'package' of know-how deliver a known result, as do, for example, consultants who design and install appraisal systems, employee incentive schemes, computerised personnel records and so on. More specifically there are people change agents, analysis change agents and organisation development agents, as shown in Box 27.

Box 27

Outside change agents

People change agents produce programmes directly affecting how people in the organisation behave; they focus on worker motivation and morale, using a variety of techniques such as management by objectives, job enrichment, reward systems and so on.

Analysis change agents concentrate on altering the technology and organisational structure to improve efficiency and output, the use of new technology or production techniques; they may also be active in forming new task groups within the organisation to install and operate innovations.

Organisation development agents examine who relates to whom, how people work together, the values and culture of the organisation, and issues such as leadership and decision-making; they may have a particular commitment to working in-depth on team and interpersonal effectiveness.

Change agents alter the *status quo* and create new situations in which people must relearn their roles. This factor alone explains why they are sometimes feared and resisted. Outsiders usually have less to lose in proposing major shifts, which is often why they are used, and there may be justification for permanent employees' fearing that their arrival heralds major cutbacks, job losses and adverse career moves.

Getting the best from an outside agent

Using an external change agent will not guarantee either comfortable or even successful results. It is therefore important to maximise the chances that a planned outside intervention will succeed. The following checklist questions can help here:

What values does the change agent hold, and will these be discussed?
A strength and weakness of outside agents is that they bring their own values to the task. It is important to clarify these values in the early stages, because they may have a fundamental impact on how the agent tackles the problem and on the agent's acceptability. For example, a catering consultant committed to the concept of privatising council services would not gain much credibility if hired by a council politically opposed to the idea.

How will conflicts between the change agent's values and those of the client be handled?
You cannot expect an outside agent to have views identical to your own or those of the organisation – there are bound to be differences. An outsider committed to achieving change primarily through involving employees may discover that the management does not value participation and is unwilling to alter its approach. How such differences are handled is as important as the existence of the differences themselves. Discover how the consultant would proceed if such differences arose. It would be unhelpful, for instance, if the consultant's approach were to press on regardless or, if faced with opposition, to resign.

What strategies will the change agent consider using?
Before signing the contract, it is important to ask the consultant how he or she would tackle your particular situation, so that you can obtain an idea of how the consultant develops a strategy for tackling problems. Are there any strategies the change agent would be reluctant or refuse to use?

A consultant will usually bring to the task a 'kit bag' of change techniques. Although there is nothing wrong with such an armoury of techniques, you may find yourself paying simply because of them. It is important that they are not applied blindly to the problem or forced to fit the situation simply because the consultant is happy using a particular tried and tested approach. For instance, a consultant with a commitment to, or experience of, appraisal systems may find it hard to avoid recommending the installation of such a system. Similarly, asked to consult on computerising some aspect of the organisation, outside computer consultants tend to favour a particular software program or piece of hardware.

How long is the change agent prepared to continue the relationship?
Consultants are usually sensitive to any suggestion that they might merely submit reports, leaving you with the problem of implementation. A simple reassurance is not enough. Spend time clarifying the time horizon of the outside change agent, and determine how far you are expecting the change agent to lead the implementation, which is primarily a management task.

Will the change agent present options for change?
There is usually more than one way of achieving a particular result and the routes by which the end is reached should be stated in terms of management choices. For example, there may be cost and human resource implications in the size and pace of a particular change. There may also be significant choices about implementation. An outside change agent examining how to introduce a computerised personnel information system, for instance, should indicate the implications of choosing between a system independent of the existing payroll suite and one based on it.

Will the change agent indicate the reasons for change and the supporting evidence?
Recommended changes should be based on evidence that can be evaluated, and the reasoning behind arriving at a particular approach should be explained.

What is the link between the change actions and the end result?
The organisation is probably paying hundreds of pounds per day for an outside agent's efforts and is entitled to see a justification for the proposals. For instance, a consultant who suggests a major programme of team-building should demonstrate first that there is a problem that demands team-building, and secondly how team-building will actually deliver the results that managers want.

Will the change agent clarify goals and objectives to all concerned?
Too often consultants talk of 'increased efficiency' or tell you that 'you will really only see the benefits in the long run', without quantifying what these notional gains will be. In the early stages of using an outside change agent, particularly ones concerned with techniques rather than process, work needs to be done to clarify roles, working procedures and expected outcomes.

Ascertain also what responsibility the outside change agent will assume for communicating goals and objectives to those who need to know. Management may leave this task to the consultant, while the latter expects managers to do it.

*What freedom will the consultant have to decide goals of change,
means of implementation, and how change will be tracked?*
Consultants or outside change agents are often presented with a broad
statement of the problem and simply asked to return with answers. This
can be costly and time-consuming if the brief is not really as open as it
is made to appear.

Leaving the implementation of change to the outsider or others
lower down in the organisation may appear to be democratic. In practice, it removes those in power from direct involvement in a process
that calls for strong guidance and actual support. Ensure that those call-
ing in the consultants stay closely in touch with the change effort.

Ask for references and follow these up
Enquire about the change agent's record of cost against estimate; about
the relationship with internal people; whether there is a tendency to
introduce inexperienced learners once the contract is landed; and
whether other clients would use the outsider again.

Of particular concern is how the change agent handles matters of
confidentiality. Does the change agent, for example, understand the
limits of the brief? One firm that hired a consultant from a well-known
institute found that the consultant also brought in two less experienced
colleagues. The latter decided to write a supplementary and unre-
quested report on problems that they had identified in how the organisation operated. This report was presented without the agreement of the
organisation's project manager, and caused considerable dismay over
its contents. The two inexperienced change agents had behaved unethi-
cally and, when confronted, did not really understand the limits of their
remit.

Change agent principles

How consultants or outside change agents create change may be little
different from the way in which managers themselves proceed, except
for particular skills or know-how. The style used, though, may be different, so, in deciding whether or not to use a particular change agent,
check that they will adapt to your own organisational style and
approach. You can do this by asking for a demonstration of skills or
experience in the areas shown in Box 31.

Outside change agents, and consultants in particular, are neither as
parasitical nor as powerful as the myths about them suggest. But they
can play a key role in the management of planned, ie deliberate,
change. At some time in your management career you may have contact with outside agents, so it is worth knowing how to obtain the best
from them.

Box 28

Expected skills and experience of a competent change agent

- Sensitive to the needs and views of those they seek to change through give and take in relationships; provides information; appreciates problems; open and willing to receive new inputs; a non-threatening personality.

- Institutionalises change by building it into the system so that a vacuum does not occur when the change agent leaves.

- Always seeks the simplest solution to achieving change; has realistic expectations.

- Aware and tolerant of the change situation.

- Operates well under stress without becoming defensive when confronted; can present differences and handle these well.

- Defines change in an attractive way to those on the receiving end

- Works through opinion leaders.

- Maximises co-operation by conveying the idea that those on the receiving end have some freedom of choice in relating to the change agent.

- Involves those on the receiving end of change with problem definition and specification of need.

- Delivers benefits; solves problems; and significantly improves situations.

GUIDELINES

- *Clarify* the values held by the change agent.

- *Agree* how conflicts between the values of the change agent and those of the client will be handled.

- *Determine* how the outside agent would go about tackling the particular situation.

- *Discover* whether there are any strategies the change agent would be reluctant or refuse to use.

- *State* the time horizon for the work of the outside change agent.

- *Resolve* how far you are expecting the change agent to lead the implementation of change.

- *Ensure* that the way in which the end result is to be achieved is subject to management choices.

- *Seek* enough information to understand why recommended changes are made and the link between them and the end result.

- *Clarify* with the outside agent roles, working procedures and expected outcomes.

- *Define* the responsibility for communicating goals and objectives to those who need to know.

- *Determine* what freedom the outside agent will have to decide change goals; means of implementation; and how change will be tracked.

- *Ask* for references and follow these up.

- *Check* that the outside agent has the required skills and experience, as shown in Box 28.

14 Tracking

Organisational change is generally difficult and frequently expensive. We invest enormous resources in the process and yet, all too often, we are unsure what has been delivered. At best, managers tend to rely on anecdote and unsubstantiated guesswork. At worst, they may prefer not to probe more deeply, perhaps suspecting that all the effort and investment have been in vain.

Nevertheless, many organisations are beginning to seek more reliable data on the impact of their change initiatives. When the food company McVitie's underwent a major restructuring a few years ago, it followed up the exercise, 12 months on, with a detailed evaluation review based on a mixture of hard performance data and more qualitative management opinion. Royal Mail – and subsequently its sister business, ParcelForce – also used sophisticated evaluation techniques to follow up major organisational change.

Monitoring and evaluation

When we track the change effort we are monitoring and evaluating. Monitoring is a continuous process of discovering what is happening, what is going off track, what people think, what needs doing next and so on. It is relatively low key and usually relies on limited information.

By contrast, evaluation is infrequent and more judgemental. It generally requires extensive information from, for example, existing and new record systems, structured and unstructured interviews, observations and so on. Specialists may be needed to organise the evaluation, make judgements about outcomes, assess how well something was done and how to do better next time. Because of the information demands, the need for rigorous analysis and the complexity of the task, evaluations can be expensive and time-consuming, and may raise more questions than they answer.

Whether you are attempting monitoring or evaluating, tracking change seeks to answer:

• What is happening?

- Did we do what we said we would do?

- What can we learn from how we did it?

- Where do we go from here?

What is happening?

Napoleon claimed that no plan survives the battle. With organisational change reality also ensures unexpected, perhaps unwanted, outcomes. Some of these may be minimised, even avoided, if corrective action is taken at the right time. So tracking is concerned with outcomes and also with discovering what is happening during the entire change process. The change process is shown in Figure 16. Tracking allows managers to review how the change is going, right from its inception through to the adjustments that inevitably occur once change is underway.

Figure 16

The change process

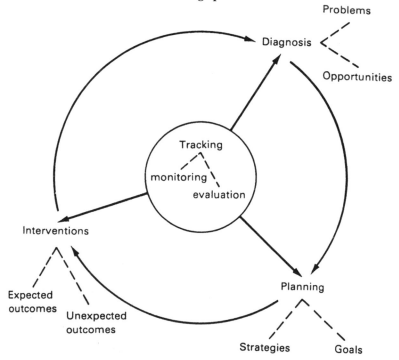

If tracking is to be useful, you need to know in advance what ought to be happening. Thus, for instance, had the Philips' management team found that the utilisation of resources was actually worsening, it would have suggested new corrective action. Knowing what ought to happen stems from being clear about the desired end state.

Did we do what we said we would do?

Most change efforts begin with no clear sense of direction, progress to weak plans and are characterised by excessive optimism about the results. More than half of all new technology projects, for example, fail to deliver the benefits expected; the bulk of company takeovers produce fewer gains than originally envisaged; and most restructuring seems to damage somebody.

Evaluation of outcomes can be worthless, however, if managers are too far into the next change effort, or if it would be too difficult to unravel the past. Evaluation may even be damaging to the actual change process. If you keep pulling up a plant to check whether its roots are growing you can hardly expect it to survive!

Evaluating outcomes to learn whether 'we did what we said we would do' is worth attempting if:

● the original change objectives were reasonably clear

● enough people want to know the results

● it is feasible and economic

● it will help dispel the myth that the change effort has failed

● the results might suggest what to do next.

Objectives
It is one of the myths of managing major change that the objectives have to be tightly specified and (preferably) quantitative. This is not confirmed by successful change-oriented organisations, particularly those good at innovating. Change objectives merely need to be clear, understandable and capable of being related to outcomes so that managers can answer the question 'Have we succeeded or failed?'

People want to know
Enough people in the organisation must want the evaluation results to justify its time and expense. Often managers would rather not probe too deeply into the change effort in case the answers they uncover are

unwelcome. Usually what will sway people to back an evaluation programme is whether the results of evaluation will be available soon
enough to guide future action. In Philips, for instance, evaluating past
changes was recognised as essential if new directions were to be identified and made acceptable across the organisation.

Feasible

The viability, timing and cost of an evaluation effort must all be right.
First, an evaluation must be possible to undertake. Given the complexity
of many change efforts, evaluation may not prove practical. Secondly,
an evaluation must begin at the right time. If it is started too early in
the change process, there will be no way of deciding whether 'we have
done what we said we would do': on the other hand, waiting until the
change effort has almost been forgotten undermines evaluation. The
best timing is when the answers arrive in time to influence future decisions. Thirdly, the costs must be acceptable for the return expected
from the evaluation.

Myths

When a change effort is undertaken there will always be those who
remain convinced that the old ways were better and who prefer the *status
quo*. It may also take a considerable time before all the benefits from the
change begin to show. Consequently, individuals or groups may persist
in looking backwards to the period before the change. The idea may pre-
vail that somehow the change has not been a success. In these circumstances, evaluation can be some help in demonstrating the reality and
identifying where the change has produced worthwhile results.

Results suggest what to do next

Worthwhile evaluation must point to future action, being a baseline
from which to decide new courses of action. For example, if a firm discovers that, having sought to capture 50 per cent of a market, it has
only acquired a third; then an analysis of the reason for its partial success may offer guidance for corrective action. Evaluation helps us to:

Avoid making that mistake again!

Learn how to repeat our successes!

Knowing what went wrong with a particular change effort, and why,
may prevent us making the same mistake twice. For example, one
company conducted an evaluation into its recent restructuring and
learned that late into the change effort an extensive team-building
effort had been required to handle problems created by the new struc-

ture. Team-building should have occurred much earlier but, having learned this, the company never repeated the mistake.

When a change effort has been highly successful, evaluation can be an investment in learning how to repeat it. For instance, an analysis of the restructuring of roles within one company showed that people liked the new arrangements and felt that the transition stage had been about the right length, removing damaging uncertainty. This provided a useful indicator for future changes in respect of timing and the transition stage.

Openly asking 'What can we learn from how we did it?' conveys the message that management is listening to what people think, inspiring confidence in the next round of changes.

Where do we go from here?

Evaluation helps decide what to do next by revealing whether the change effort is on course. Since organisational goals are continually changing, it may be relevant at any time during the change process. It is more important to establish what to do next than to conduct a perfect evaluation. Driving many organisational changes is a management vision of the future. Evaluation shows whether the organisation is still moving towards this vision or whether the pace is slowing.

A plan

Having decided to evaluate a change effort, how do you go about it? Because change efforts vary so widely it is only possible to identify the broad outline of what should happen, as shown in Box 29.

Box 29

Creating an evaluation plan
STEP 1   DEFINE 'the customer' – who 'owns' responsibility for acting on the eventual results?
STEP 2   CLARIFY purpose or priorities for evaluation, ensure 'customer' agreement
STEP 3   DECIDE when to evaluate, methods of data collection and analysis
STEP 4   SPECIFY and commit resources needed and available, and role of staff
STEP 5   DETERMINE information required and sources
STEP 6   LIST who will receive data from evaluation

Figure 17

Stream analysis

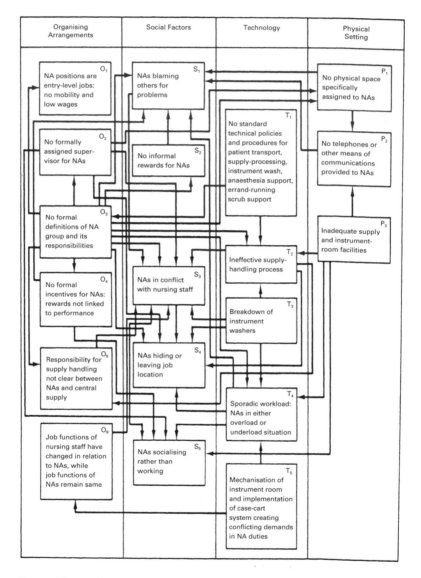

Source: J Porras, *Stream Analysis*, © 1987, Addison-Wesley Publishing Co., Inc., Reading, Massachusetts. Reprinted with permission.

Tracking, particularly evaluation, produces large amounts of data which managers must analyse and interpret. It is extremely useful to have a road map to guide the process. One such is called stream analysis.

Stream analysis

Stream analysis is the invention of Dr Jerry Porras, consultant and associate professor at Stanford University. Using charts to show what is happening at any time during the change effort, stream analysis assumes that organisations consist of different, but interconnected subsystems.

As Chapter 1 on Models indicates, it can be difficult to make sense of all the relationships produced by seeing the organisation as an open system. Even so, stream analysis tries to chart the interconnections. It can be used by a single manager or (preferably) a small team responsible for guiding the change effort. Four components lie at the heart of stream analysis, and are the setting in which change occurs:

- organisational arrangements

- social factors

- technology

- physical setting.

Organisational problems are collected and allocated to one of these four settings. Attempts are made to trace the links by examining whether one problem seems to be causing another; whether one problem is related to another with no evidence of a causal link; whether a problem both causes and is caused by another; and whether there is a clear and reasonably significant relationship between one problem and another.

Stream analysis was applied by a manager in a large community hospital that had been expanding fast for six years and was experiencing problems with its nursing assistants (NAs). Absenteeism existed, turnover was high, and job performance was poor. Persistent issues needing a concerted attack are highlighted in Figure 17.

Lack of adequate technical standards and procedures emerged as a core issue, along with three other slightly less critical ones. Instead of making scapegoats of the NAs, the causes of the human problems were identified. An action plan was devised and implemented, the changes being tracked using the stream analysis technique.

The steps for conducting stream analysis are shown in Box 30. They offer managers a practical way of tracking change and uncovering what has been done, so that the organisation can learn how to change itself more effectively.

Box 30

> ### *Stream analysis steps*
>
> 1 Form a change management team
> 2 Collect information on issues in the organisation
> 3 Categorise and place issues on a stream chart
> 4 On the chart draw interconnections among issues
> 5 Analyse and identify core problems, stories and themes
> 6 Create a stream planning chart to guide actions prescribed by the diagnosis
> 7 Implement the plan
> 8 Document intervention activity on a stream tracking chart

GUIDELINES

- *Distinguish* between monitoring or evaluating the change effort.

- *Set* clear change objectives to assist in tracking.

- *Use* the four tracking questions:
  What is happening?
  Did we do what we said we would do?
  What can we learn from how we did it?
  Where do we go from here?

- *Consider* tracking only if:
  the answer might suggest what to do next
  change objectives were reasonably clearly specified
  enough people want the results
  it is feasible and economic
  it will help dispel the myth that the change effort has failed.

- *Develop* a systematic evaluation plan.

- *Try* using stream analysis to unravel the complexities of the change effort.

15   Force-field analysis

Force-field analysis (FFA) helps analyse situations that you want to change. Using it, you can tackle seemingly immovable obstacles to change. The technique has been around for decades, outlasting many other management aids. As a tool of great resilience, it continues to be taught on management courses.

Generations of working managers have found FFA simple to understand, easy to use and effective. It starts by assuming that:

At any given moment, any situation in an organisation is in a state of equilibrium.

This is a version of the physical sciences' law that a body will be at rest when all the forces acting on it cancel each other out. It does not mean that everything is locked into a static state or permanent *status quo*. In an organisation there is dynamic tension between a whole set of counteracting forces that maintain the *status quo* (see Figure 18).

Some of the forces push towards goal achievement; others oppose it. Suppose that some specialist staff in an organisation decide that they should be paid more. They have many forces pushing them to obtain this goal, such as extra work being thrust on them, longer working hours, market demand for their skills, family pressures, inflation and so on. There may be equally strong counter-forces, such as the wish of management to restrain further wage rises, the wish of other staff to preserve differentials, the desire not to let this group of specialists become too important, and so on.

Change is possible only when one or both of the following occur:

Restraining forces weaken

Driving forces strengthen.

There are, consequently, two distinct if sometimes complementary routes to making things happen. It may be feasible to strengthen the driving forces pushing the situation towards a particular goal. For instance, the specialists in the above example might make themselves even more indispensable by taking on important new roles or projects.

Figure 18

Analysing the forces

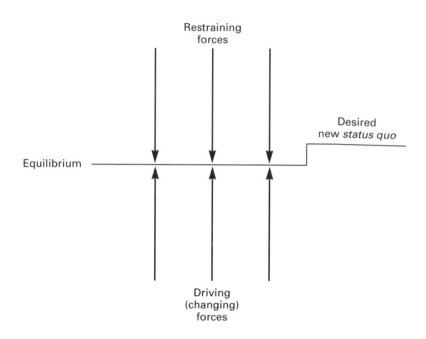

If it is impossible to increase the driving forces, then perhaps it may be feasible to weaken the restraining forces that are preventing change In the above example, the specialists might let it be known that they are all job-hunting, which may weaken management's resolve to resist change. Or the managers might strengthen the resisting forces by limiting dependence on the specialists by subcontracting some work to outside suppliers.

When the equilibrium of driving and restraining forces is disturbed (ie the forces become out of balance), change occurs towards, or away from, the desired goal. Once this happens, the situation may continue moving in unexpected ways by:

A return to the previous *status quo*

Reaching some entirely different goal.

The management of change first requires an unfreezing of the balanced set of forces maintaining the *status quo*, then, with the establishment of a new and desired equilibrium, making it permanent or refreezing. Otherwise, powerful forces may undermine the change, causing a return to the old *status quo*. The process is shown in simplified form in Figure 19 below:

Figure 19

Making change stick

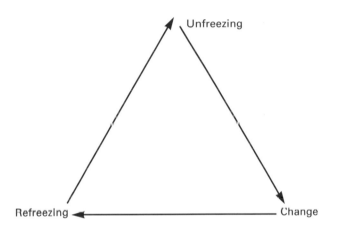

For example, when a manager or outside change agent who has introduced important organisational changes departs, there may be powerful forces that gradually reverse the changes, unless they have been 'frozen' into place.

This view of the change as a process of unfreezing and then refreezing is less acceptable today, because we are more conscious of the dynamics of the change process. New equilibriums are rare in a period of great change. Situations are constantly altering, and the aim of refreezing, although attractive, is unrealistic. Force-field analysis does, however, provide a useful way of focusing attention on the power of driving and restraining forces.

Diagnosis

Using FFA is a combination of defining the problem or situation, carefully followed by reviewing the driving and restraining forces to see how to affect them. The power of FFA lies in affecting at least one of the forces. The main steps in using FFA are summarised below.

Figure 20

Analysing the forces

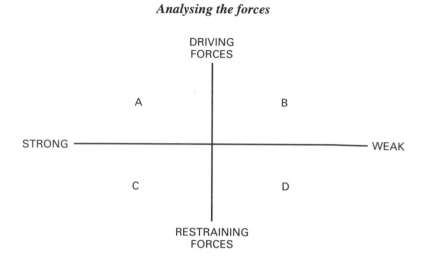

Step 1   State the problem area

Define the broad topic area, such as issues concerned with personnel, marketing, production, administration and so on. The problem must be a real one, important to you and worth trying to resolve. The problem area defines the boundaries of the situation that you want to alter.

Step 2   Define the situation

Next state the situation to be changed in order to describe the *status quo*. For example, a group of foremen may make a problem area statement that they are concerned about output quality. To define the situation they go further and state specifically that the present reject rate of 20 per cent is unacceptable.

Because a problem defined is often a problem half-solved, it pays to spend time producing a tight specification of the situation. How big is the problem, how important is it, where is it located, who or what is involved with it, was there a time when the problem did not exist?

Step 3   Specify the goal

Now you define the new situation that you want to reach. This is a goal, a statement of how the situation would look if the blocks to change were removed and a new *status quo* was achieved.

It can be helpful to express the goal in quantified form, or at least provide some measurable way of deciding whether the goal has actually been achieved. In the above example, the foreman decide that their goal is to achieve zero defects. Defining both the *status quo* and the goal produces a picture of the gap due to the current equilibrium of driving and restraining forces.

Step 4   Analyse the forces

Now create two separate lists showing restraining and driving forces. These lists may come from a mixture of brainstorming and more detailed research. You are only interested in forces already at work, not ones that might arise in the future or have ceased to exist. You can also classify each force into: strong; medium; or weak. The information will fall into four main types as shown in Figure 20.

This analysis should allow you to decide where to begin affecting the *status quo* by influencing the various forces. You may, for instance, conclude that it is better to affect those falling in area A rather than waste time on those in area B. Similarly, you may conclude that restraining forces in area C are too difficult to influence and that it is more sensible to spend time weakening forces in area D.

In defining the forces you need to be specific. A statement such as 'Opposition from senior management' may need refining into 'The assistant chief executive opposes the project'. Or 'Lack of regular feedback' may need hardening to 'We never receive praise when we do things well.'

When describing a complicated force, you may need to break it down into its components, to make it easier to decide what might be done. For example, a restraining force such as 'Poor marketing support' may need subdividing into 'Irregular market surveys'; 'Marketing department not in regular contact'; 'Marketing director gives weak support to experimenting with new promotional ideas'.

To examine the various forces in further depth, you can also categorise them into:

- *Personal forces* – anything that refers to you, such as attitudes, feelings, weaknesses, relationships, education, income and so on

- *Relationship forces* – how different individuals and groups relate to each other, such as the organisation and government, the department and other departments, the team and other teams and so on

- *System forces* – factors that form the organisation's environment, including political, social, legal, environmental, local conditions and so on.

It is helpful to draw a visual impression of the various forces pushing for and against change. For example, Figure 21 shows an analysis of a situation in the welfare field. The *problem area* is inter-agency planning and provision of services for carers (that is people who look after elderly or handicapped relatives at home).

Figure 21

FFA in action

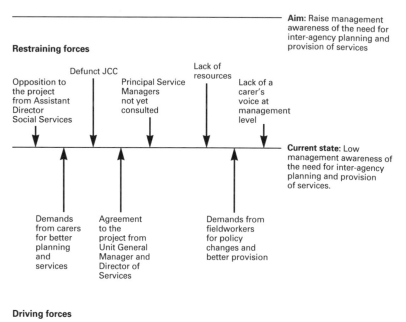

Source: *Action for Carers*, Kings Fund, 1988

The *definition of the situation* is the low management awareness of the need for inter-agency planning and provision of services; the *goal* is to raise awareness about it. The various restraining and driving forces are shown at the head of each arrow. A further sophistication would be to vary the lengths of the arrows to reflect the strength or weakness of the forces that they represent.

Step 5 Devise a strategy

Think carefully about your strategy for altering the *status quo*. For instance, by increasing driving forces that threaten or pressure people, you may increase resistance to altering the *status quo*. You rarely have enough time or knowledge to influence all the forces – nor is this necessary. With the situation in equilibrium, and driving forces exactly matching restraining forces, all you need to locate is one force susceptible to your influence. This is like an army commander probing for the enemy's weak spot. It is seldom necessary to find more than one. Thus, you choose the force that is easiest to change and has the best result.

It is generally better to strengthen those driving forces that do not increase resistance; or to work to weaken restraining forces; or to consider how new driving forces can be brought into play. Also consider tackling forces that cause the least disruption when altered.

The best strategy may prove to be a dual one: to weaken restraining and to strengthen driving forces, particularly if you are not sure about the relative importance of the various forces.

Step 6 Develop an action plan

Once you have decided on a strategy for affecting one or more of the forces, you need a detailed plan of action. This may consist of many highly practical tasks, and these must be treated like any other management aim, in which there is clarity about who will do what, when, and the resources needed to make each task possible. There should also be some criteria by which you can decide whether the task has been completed or not.

Keep the various steps in your action plan simple. Go for many small successes rather than a single large one. To influence one of the driving or restraining forces, your action plan must be followed through with determination, and you should always be able to tell whether your individual small steps are succeeding or failing.

Step 7 Establish a new equilibrium

Once you have influenced the driving or restraining forces, change is set in motion. Now there is the possibility that events may take an unexpected turn, the original goal being reached and left behind, or an entirely new and perhaps undesirable situation being created. An example of this latter situation is a company that makes a much-publicised takeover bid for another firm and, having succeeded, finds itself on the receiving end of unwelcome offers.

Once a new situation has been achieved, there is a risk of returning to the previous *status quo* unless the changes are made irreversible. The implication of using FFA (see below) is that efforts must be made to consolidate the change, to refreeze the situation and to create a new, acceptable *status quo*. This may be harder than the original task of disturbing the equilibrium. To institutionalise change, you have to ensure that the new situation becomes part of the fabric of the organisation itself.

An example of refreezing a situation is when a manager finds ways to make people 'own' the changes and have a vested interest in maintaining the new situation. If, for instance, a manager introduces a new statistical reporting system for monitoring progress and insists that every month the output from the system is reviewed, this builds it into people's regular thinking habits and work roles.

Why use FFA?

Force-field analysis (FFA) provides a simple framework to help people decide what steps they ought to take. Another of its benefits is that it reduces a problem to a 'do-able' size. It also stimulates new ways of taking action. If certain situations seem set in concrete with little likelihood for change, FFA can encourage a more optimistic view, directing a search for those vulnerable points where the right action will tip the balance, starting a move away from the present *status quo*.

A further attraction of FFA is that it can be used by an individual manager or by a large group. The latter will often prove more creative than a person working alone. It assists a group to get on the same wavelength, reach a common understanding of a situation, develop a sense of teamwork and make a commitment to the change goal.

Effective though FFA can be it depends for its success on the quality and completeness of the analysis. For example, if you fail to identify all the main driving and restraining forces, you may be faced with selecting one to alter that is particularly difficult, when in fact there are easier, unlisted, ones available.

Finally, the clear framework for developing an action plan that is the strength of FFA is also its weakness. On occasions it can seem over-analytical and elaborate. Despite this, it is a proven aid that can considerably improve the quality of thinking and planning that goes into the change effort.

GUIDELINES

- *Create* separate lists of restraining and driving forces.

- *Break* down complicated situations into their components with their own driving and restraining forces.

- *Analyse forces* into whether they deal with personal factors, relationships or systems.

- *Draw* a visual representation of the various forces involved in maintaining a situation.

- *Focus* effort and resources on affecting one force, the 'weak spot', in the situation.

- *Keep* action plans simple.

- *Seek* to refreeze, to institutionalise, the new situation.

16   Other facilitation tools

Diagnostic tools

Although force-field analysis (FFA), as described in Chapter 15, can be a powerful tool for facilitating change, its value ultimately depends on the quality and completeness of the analysis supporting it. For example, if you fail to identify all the main driving or restraining forces, you may end up struggling to deal with a particularly problematic factor, when there are other, less challenging influences that might have been addressed. Equally, if you fail to identify a significant restraining force, you may find that, although you have expended substantial energy on dealing with the factors identified, you are still unable to implement the required change.

To help overcome these problems, the value of FFA can be further enhanced by combining it with other tools, particularly during the diagnostic or analytical phases. Many of these tools are already familiar to organisations involved in total quality management (TQM) or problem-solving initiatives, but they remain useful weapons in the change armoury.

The key here is the accurate identification of both the nature of the issue addressed and the various factors likely to influence it. A recurrent problem in many organisations is the temptation to jump very quickly into 'solution mode'. We think that we understand the nature of the problem addressed, so we start immediately trying to develop solutions. All too often, the problem itself has been misunderstood or misdiagnosed, and so we end up developing an inappropriate solution. Similarly, in using FFA, we jump to conclusions about what are likely to be the driving or restraining forces, and so we expend considerable energy in trying to influence factors that, in practice, prove to be relatively unimportant.

In preparing to use FFA, therefore, or indeed in preparing for any change process, it is often worth investing significant time in ensuring that you genuinely understand the issues to be addressed. One of the truisms about change management is that the secret is in the preparation. Figure 22, for instance, illustrates one organisation's view of the 'ideal' approach to change management, based on the allocation of time and resources to the various phases of the project:

Figure 22

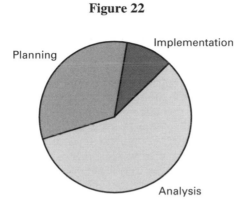

The proportions in Figure 22 are simply illustrative, but the message is clear. The first priority is effective analysis of the issues to be addressed, and the second is the planning of the changes. If those two elements are carried out effectively, then implementation becomes relatively straightforward. Although this view may be rather simplistic in practice (not least because in implementing change, the devil is all too often in the unexpected detail), the principle is undoubtedly right. Effective change, and effective use of FFA to support it, depends on a thorough understanding of the issues involved prior to taking action.

Diagnosing the problem

The first step, then, is to ensure that we genuinely understand the issue that is being addressed. In practice, it is often difficult to persuade managers to take the required step back to analyse the nature of the issue: they know they have a problem, and they generally have a pretty good idea of what the problem is, and they may therefore be reluctant to 'waste' time in further analysis. And yet, very often, the real problem may be quite different from that perceived. One company, for instance, perceived difficulties in recruiting call-centre staff, and – jumping straight to a solution – made some rapid increases in entry salaries, only to find that the problem became worse. On reflection, it became evident that the real problem was the retention of existing staff, and that recruitment was a problem only because of the very high levels of turnover. By increasing entry salaries, the company had simply increased the dissatisfaction of the rest of the workforce, and so raised turnover still higher. Having identified the real problem, the company was then able to take steps to address the retention issues.

Various techniques can be used to help analyse the nature of the issue, including the tools described in Chapter 17 on Sensing and Surveys. It is often the case, for example, that management perspectives on the issues are significantly detached from those of the workforce, which in itself may be a cause of misdiagnosis.

Another useful tool is the 'is/is not' review, which simply involves key players in trying to separate factors that are part of the problem from those that are not. On the surface, this sounds a simple process. In practice, it is often very challenging, because it involves being very precise about the nature of the problem and about our priorities for addressing it. In particular, it involves separating the factors that we wish to address from those that we see either as not part of the problem or as low-priority. Overall, our aim is to crystallise a precise definition of the problem from the mass of data available to us.

To do this, we gather the managers involved together in a workshop format and ask them to identify the factors that they see as part of the problem to be addressed, and those factors that we might reasonably expect to be part of the issue but that are not (or that are seen as relatively unimportant). This can be done against a number of dimensions, including:

- time (ie when does the issue occur and when does it not?)

- place (ie where does it occur and when not?)

- people (ie does it affect some but not others?)

- technology or equipment (ie is some involved and not others?)

- processes (ie are some involved and not others?).

The technique is best illustrated through an example. In a manufacturing operation, for instance, we may have identified a quality problem, such as an unacceptably high level of defects in the end-product. Our first reaction might be to conduct a thorough overall analysis of the whole production process. The use of an 'is/is not' review, on the other hand, might quickly identify the real nature of the problem. If we bring together managers or operators from various stages from the production process, we may find that, for example, the problem is only evident at particular times or at a particular stage in the process. We might find that it occurs on some production lines but not others, or at some points in the day but not others. All of these factors will provide clues to the real nature of the problem, and will therefore mean that we can focus our responses much more precisely.

Most commonly, these techniques will enable us to distil an apparently all-embracing issue into a precise and manageable set of requirements. In the above case, for example, it might translate 'We have a problem with production quality' into 'We have some specific technology problems at these particular points on production lines 2 and 4.' It may also help to refocus our attention. In the case cited earlier, this process might take the company from 'We have a problem with recruitment' to 'We have a problem retaining staff, particularly at grade 4 with less than 2 years' service, in these particular locations.' We might also decide that, although some elements are apparently part of the problem, they are of relatively low priority: for instance, we might decide to address particularly high turnover at one location and give less attention to turnover issues elsewhere.

In carrying out the 'is/is not' review, it is critical to ensure that all relevant parties are involved and that data is gathered from all pertinent sources. If the issue has staffing or human resource implications, it will often be necessary to gather employee views of the problem, perhaps using sensing or survey techniques. Similarly, if the issue has customer implications, it may be useful to gather customer feedback and feed this into the discussion. The key here is to ensure that the input is representative. We may, for example, interpret a small number of customer complaints as indicative of a wide-ranging problem, whereas a more representative view might indicate that the issue is more specific.

Identifying possible causes

The 'is/is not' review will help us to identify, as precisely as possible, the nature of the issue to be addressed. At its conclusion, we should have established a very precise definition of what we are dealing with – specifying such details as where, when, who and what is involved. The next step in planning our change process is to identify the range of factors contributing to the issue: in other words, what do we need to change?

The most common tool for identifying contributory factors is the Ishikawa or 'fishbone' diagram, which sets out possible factors under a series of headings, as illustrated in Figure 23.

Figure 23

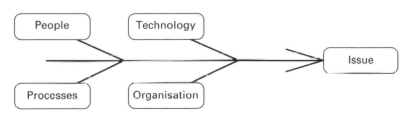

The specific headings can be amended to suit the situation or the organisation, although the above are perhaps those most commonly used to structure the thinking of participants. Again, this technique is most effectively used in a workshop format, with the participation of a representative group of those involved in the issue. This might involve both direct participants and those on the receiving end – notably, internal or external customers. These groups may often have useful perspectives on the issues involved.

In the first instance, participants simply brainstorm possible contributory factors under the various headings. It is generally useful to apply brainstorming 'rules' initially: that is, participants must not question or challenge the causes that are being proposed. This helps to promote a creative approach to identifying factors and encourages participants to consider factors that may be outside their usual assumptions. One of the major benefits of this approach is that it can help to identify factors that might previously have been disregarded.

Once the group has produced an initial list of possible factors under each heading, these can then be developed and debated in detail. First, it is important to ensure that each suggestion is fully understood by the group, which may often involve developing a one-word suggestion into a more detailed outline. If, for instance, we think that staff motivation may be a factor, what do we mean by this? Which staff? What affects their motivation? What impact does this have? In each case, the group should probe the suggestion in detail, making sure that its meaning is fully clear to everyone.

The second stage is to assess whether the proposed factor really does contribute to the issue. This may often involve further research outside the group. It is critical that the group does not jump to conclusions but is prepared to obtain more information and reconvene if necessary. If we think that employee motivation may be a factor, we may need to speak to employees to see whether this is the case.

Finally, once we have identified those factors that appear to be contributing, we can then prioritise them in terms of their perceived impact on the issue in question. Two factors are likely to be critical here, as illustrated in the Johari window shown in Figure 24. In terms of influencing our change activity, our priority will be to deal with the factors in the top right-hand box – that is, the ones that are likely to have greatest impact on the issue but that can be changed most easily. We can then move on to those aspects that are high-impact, but more difficult to influence. Overall, this process will help us to structure our plans for change so that we focus our resources most effectively in meeting the precise needs we have identified.

Figure 24

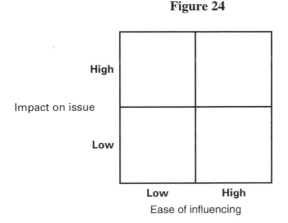

Impact on issue

High

Low

Low   High

Ease of influencing

GUIDELINES

- *Enhance* the value of FFA further by combining it with other tools, particularly during the diagnostic or analytical phases

- *Identify* accurately the nature of the issue being addressed and the various factors likely to influence it; effective change management depends on this

- *Avoid* the temptation to jump too quickly into 'solution mode', invest significant time to ensure that you genuinely understand the issues to be addressed

- *Use* sensing or survey techniques to help your understanding of the problem, or use the 'is/is not' review to help separate factors that are part of the problem from those that are not; ensure that all relevant parties are involved and that the data is gathered from all pertinent sources

- *Try* the Ishikawa or 'fishbone' diagram to help identify contributory factors; don't jump to conclusions, but instead be prepared to seek more information if necessary

- *Prioritise* the contributory factors you have identified in terms of their perceived impact on the issue in question and in terms of the ease with which they can be influenced

17   Sensing and surveys

'You need to get under the skin of this organisation'; 'One never really knows what people think in this place'; 'I don't have enough contact yet with people in this organisation'; 'Recognising the need to change must go beyond just me'; 'I need some hard data on which to base changes'; 'I must find a way to get my influential senior colleagues convinced of the need for change'; 'I want to tap people's ideas.'

These are just some of the ways in which organisational leaders express the challenge of organisational change. In the cycle of strategic change (see Figure 2, Chapter 1 on Models) the first issue is:

What changes do we need to make – diagnosis?

The greater your power and responsibility, the less daily contact you will usually have with people doing much of the work – the ones who make your ideas succeed. How can you discover what changes they consider relevant?

Ways to diagnose what changes are needed include employee attitude surveys, polling, feedback through the managment hierarchy on specific issues, suggestion schemes, market research, and so on. Management by walking around can also be revealing.

There are occasions, though, when you want to tap systematically into a wide range of views about possible organisational change without using the clinical approach of formal surveys or leaving it to individualistic approaches such as management by walking around. *Sensing* is a way of learning from people in the organisation with whom there is little personal contact. As a diagnostic tool, it highlights issues, rather than suggesting how to deal with them. The two main ways of sensing are:

- *vertical sensing* – usually conducted in small groups from an entire vertical slice of the organisation

- *horizontal sensing* – using participants from no more than three or four levels across the entire organisation.

188

The aim is to identify problems of concern to the chosen groups, whether they be supervisors, middle managers, front-line staff, accountants, engineers and so on.

Sensing in action

John Mortimer is general manager of a company employing around 1,500 people. He has produced a clear statement explaining his vision of what sort of organisation he wants it to become. His business plan focuses on expanding exports, and he particularly wants to uncover ways of improving the company's general performance. He needs the commitment of his senior managers and the rest of their staff if the vision and business plan are to become a reality. He is acutely aware that an upward flow of unfiltered information is hard to achieve. It is easier to send information downwards than to draw it from below.

Achieving any organisational change requires energy and commitment. This is especially so when you are wanting to turn a general awareness of problems and opportunities into positive action Transforming a mere feeling that change is needed into a widely held view demands credible data. The act of collecting such data can itself influence people to accept that a major change is justified.

John Mortimer has heard about sensing and decides that it is appropriate for him to use. He asks his deputy to schedule 10 meetings, each 90 minutes long, with different groups of employees. To gain a 'feel' fo what people throughout the organisation think, the two managers decide to invite a mix of staff:

Group 1: Non-supervisory, technical and office employees

Group 2: Professional employees and staff specialists

Group 3: Supervisors

Group 4: Cross-sections of employees – one person from each organisational level, and no person chosen reports to any other attending.

Before scheduling the meetings, the deputy manager contacts the manager or supervisor of each person to be invited. He explains that the purpose is to help John Mortimer learn direct from employees what they think should be done to improve the company's performance so that it can become the sort of firm they have been hearing he wants to create. It is stressed that anyone attending the meeting will be talking 'off the record': no direct actions will stem from these meetings relating to the individual employee or his immediate line manager.

The initial meetings prove difficult to establish, because there is suspicion that the exercise is useless. Some managers and supervisors resent their staff's being asked to a strange meeting with the general manager without them attending too. The deputy manager uncovers another worry of middle managers and supervisors: that subordinates involved in the meetings will be leaving tasks that are equally or more important.

Resentment and distrust make John Mortimer realise that he must spend more time discussing, presenting and gaining commitment to the project. To achieve this, he creates a small project team of managers drawn from across the whole spectrum of the firm. The deputy general manager is made responsible for ensuring that ideas flowing from the sensing exercise are followed through, underlining top management's commitment to the process. This begins to build confidence that it will be more than a talking-shop.

Meetings of the project team with the general manager confirm and disseminate the message that he is genuinely interested in learning what people are thinking. This knowledge permeates the organisation more effectively than announcements, memos or newsletters. An important task that the project team achieves is clarifying that the sensing groups are mandatory, ie those invited must attend.

The project team helps the general manager and his deputy rethink how people will be selected on a random basis: the mechanics of inviting around 120 people, the structure of the meetings, what questions will be asked, how the information will be handled and so on. The location for the meeting is carefully chosen. The general manager's office is too daunting; even another manager's office is considered unsuitable. The only other meeting rooms are too small, so the staff restaurant is adapted, screens sectioning off an area and making a pleasant informal setting.

Each meeting starts with a warm-up by the deputy manager, who again clarifies its purpose, explaining that the general manager will arrive in about half an hour. The whole event will be open and informal, and he suggests a way of treating the occasion:

Imagine that you were on a train going to visit relatives, and you happen to find yourself sitting next to the general manager. He's obviously in a mood to hear how you see things in the company at present; over a beer or a coffee you take the opportunity of telling him!

To emphasise the informality, beer, sandwiches and coffee are provided, and to create an open style of meeting, the chairs are arranged in a circle rather than around a table.

Confidentiality is also discussed. The deputy manager confirms that no actions will result from these meetings relating to individuals, their immediate line manager or supervisor. Information will be used in summary form only, not with people's named contributions. The deputy also indicates that he proposes to use a tape recorder to simplify note-taking. The general manager may also use the tapes later to refresh his memory or to present word pictures to the division's top staff. If any member of the group prefers he will immediately stop the tape now or at any time during the meeting.

A review of sensing by the project team has shown the importance of not attempting too much at each session. To prompt people to think about the issues they might want to raise, the deputy manager shows a flipchart with some appropriate prompts:

- The three things I really dislike about working here are . . .

- I really like working here because . . .

- The main ways I'd like to improve things around here are . . .

He reminds them that these are only prompts and anyone can raise anything they feel strongly about.

Although John Mortimer is forceful and self-confident, he is worried that people will close up and not talk frankly. At the suggestion of the project team, he comes armed with a few direct questions in case the meeting flags. These do not deal with general issues such as 'How can we make our firm the best in the field?' or 'How can we improve our export performance?', about which the participants may lack knowledge. Instead they are specific and allow people to use their personal experience:

- What sort of things seem to prevent you doing your job even better?

- If you had to describe in one word to the present management a way of helping you do a better job, what would it be?

- Do you get enough information to do your job well?

- What sort of things would make this an exciting, attractive place to work in each day?

Most of the people at the meeting do not know each other, or do so only slightly, but by the time the general manager arrives they are relaxed and chatting about the issues on the flipchart. When John Mortimer sits down, there is a momentary awkward silence. The conversation starts again when he smiles, helps himself to a beer and sits back looking interested. Any anxiety that he might not obtain honest opinions is quickly dispelled. What people say is usually straight from the shoulder, and often insightful to a point that surprises him. In every group there are always one or two people who moan and an even greater number who clearly have something to 'get off their chests'. Mostly, though, everyone is constructive, committed to the spirit of the sensing meeting.

A common theme that emerges in all the meetings is concern that all this talking may not lead to any changes. Certainly the sensing meeting is ripe for abuse, managers collecting quantities of information only to sink into the daily grind of keeping the organisation going – maintaining the *status quo*. When pressed on this, John Mortimer refers to the role of the deputy director who chairs the project team and confirms that there is now a task force for seeing that what emerges is turned into an action programme.

After each meeting a letter from the general manager goes to the participants thanking them for their contribution and explaining that the entire sensing exercise will be completed within two months. There will then be a four-week period of analysis followed by a review of the results by top management. Specific action is expected to start a month later. The participants also receive a brief summary of the points raised in their particular meeting without mentioning anyone's name.

The meetings with John Mortimer are spread over two months, by which time both he and the deputy director possess a huge amount of data. They are also extremely tired. Sensing is no easy option, being emotionally and physically draining, particularly if you have always to appear alert and interested in what is being said.

Data analysis is handled in several ways:

- content analysis

- impression reports by the general manager and his deputy

- analysis by type of group.

The project team undertakes the first and last of these tasks, using tape transcripts, plus the tapes themselves. The reports of the two senior managers are based on their own impressions of the meetings using their memory, notes and occasionally the tapes. Their two reports are submitted to the project team.

The project team prepares a presentation to the board of directors and a second for other groups of managers. The presentation shows the main findings, using facts and interpretation combined with actual playbacks of selected comments from the groups. The presentation is hard-hitting, specific and at times amusing, as extracts from the tapes bring colour to the points being made.

Three meetings are held to inform those who attended the original sensing meetings about the management response, and this gives participants a chance to hear about likely actions. A company newsletter is sent to every employee explaining the results and a regular bulletin is issued on how management is following through on the findings.

Although the results of the sensing exercise take time to permeate the whole organisation, everyone is soon aware of what has emerged from the meetings, together with a provisional list of proposed actions. The latter have been hammered out in the boardroom, where the top team has been confronting the more uncomfortable messages emerging from the meetings. The selected tape playbacks make an eloquent and powerful case for long-due changes, particularly those relating to management style and communications.

From John Mortimer's viewpoint, he has achieved some important results from his change effort, which are shown in Box 31.

Box 31

Results from a sensing exercise
• Hard data available about what changes are needed
• How to tackle change becomes clearer
• Senior management team and below more aware of the need to make changes
• A significant and committed core of people created who 'own' the need for changes and want to see them through
• Significant number of employees at all levels enabled to speak their minds about what changes are required
• Creative and new ideas identified to form an agenda for a longer-term change effort
• Programme of management action identified and initiated

Variations

There are many variations of sensing. It can be done on a one-to-one basis rather than in a group, and with more structured questions than used in the above example. The advantage of a group session is being able to test whether the ideas, perceptions and issues raised are commonly held. Occasionally, as with John Mortimer and his deputy, it makes sense for more than one senior person to attend, to compare notes and to watch for misunderstandings.

Sensing interviews, and even group sessions, can be conducted on the telephone. The latter rules out important non-verbal communication and is less effective than meeting face-to-face. It is also feasible, though costly, to use television conference technology to save people travelling to a particular location.

Although part of the power of sensing is that management is actually seen to be listening, it is possible to use a consultant to conduct sensing meetings. When this happens there is a risk that people will dismiss the whole exercise as a charade. However, a mixture of consultant and management-led sensing groups may prove effective. A consultant may also be able to extract more honest opinions from staff in some organisations where managers have a poor record of listening to staff views.

Finally, sensing may be spread over years rather than weeks or months. In 1980, in the US Zebco company (that specialised in making fishing reels), the vice-president of manufacturing started having two-hour meetings with employees in groups of four. He explained about the need to improve quality and the need for lower costs and, in additional plant meetings, he asked what people needed in order to do their jobs better. It took two years for the vice-president to meet all the employees.

Questions

The use of direct questions in sensing has to be considered carefully. It may prove overwhelming, and rapport should be established before presenting direct questions to groups. The sequence of questions should also be adapted to the local situation. A basic structure for helping to formulate questions is shown in Box 32.

Devising questions for sensing meetings is relatively easy. The skill is to use them sparingly, without creating communication blocks or causing people to withhold. The phrasing of the questions as well as their delivery should be non-threatening and it is also worth checking that each question is fully understood (see also Chapter 20 on Verbal Skills).

Box 32

Structure for formulating sensing questions

- ROLES – for example, what do you do, what are your responsibilities; how would you describe your job to someone else; are you clear how you fit into the organisation?

- GOALS – for example, what are your short-term goals for your job right now; what should the organisation do to help you achieve these goals; do you have any long-term career goals; what work would you like to be doing next in this organisation?

- YOUR JOB – for example, what are the good things and the bad things about your job; what parts of the job seem important to you; what parts of your job seem a waste of time; what extra responsibility might you have that you do not have now; is there anything you do that should be done by someone else; to do your job well do you feel supported and informed by managers?

- ORGANISATION – for example, what is it about this organisation that helps you to be effective; what things around here make you less than fully effective; why is it worth coming to work here; why do people stay here for many years; why do people leave?

- RELATIONSHIPS – for example, how would you describe your relationship with your immediate boss and with the person above the boss; what are their respective strengths and weaknesses; what kind of relations do you have with people at the same level in the organisation; how would you describe these people; what kind of subordinates do you have and how effective are your relationships with them?

- YOUR TEAM – for example, what are the major problems facing your work team right now; how are decisions made in your team; how supportive is your team when you have a problem; does your team regularly review its effectiveness and what it is trying to achieve?

- CHANGES – for example, what changes should your immediate boss make right now; what changes should the senior management make; what should change in your team; in what way would you like to see those who report direct to you change; what changes should you be making right now?

- HERE AND NOW – what do you think about this meeting, interview, discussion etc; what do you think about the organiser of this meeting; what do you think the organiser of the meeting is feeling or thinking; what do you feel about the person holding this meeting?

The pros and cons

Some of the benefits from sensing were revealed when John Mortimer used it (see above). The more general pros and cons are summrised in

Box 33. It has an immediate appeal for some managers and in an adapted form is used by many consultants. It demands a significant commitment of time and resources.

Box 33

Pros and cons of sensing	
PROS	CONS
UNDERSTANDING – a chance to check out what people feel and say	EXPENSE – demanding of time, space and staff (but can still be more economical than individual interviews)
AMPLIFICATION – comments can be elaborated and expanded	
DISCOVERY – unknown problems can be uncovered	GOALS – not always shared or understood
SUPPLEMENTING – can support and supplement data gathered from other sources	ANALYSIS – data can be difficult and time-consuming to analyse or summarise; data may be lost in the vast amount of information generated
LANGUAGE – is that of the participant, not the manager; makes the results more acceptable	THREAT – anxiety-creating for some participants; unless understood by line managers can be resisted strongly; usefulness limited if lack of trust exists between individuals at different levels in the organisation; some people may feel they are being spied on
CREDIBILITY – data gathered this way is often more credible than that gathered through other means	
CONTACT – provides an opportunity for personal contact between change agent and others	
OPENNESS – when people feel they are being understood they are more open	ACCESS – requires people to be brought together who may be spread across different locations
RAPPORT – easier than some other methods to establish rapport between participants and manager, hence more openness and useful information gained	

Overall, sensing is an extremely effective mechanism for providing an insight into the nature and range of issues that are present in the organisation, and so helps management to decide what kinds of changes are needed (and, indeed, what factors are likely to impede or facilitate change).

However, although sensing provides highly detailed information about issues and opinions within the organisation, it does not, in itself, provide any reliable means of quantifying the depth or strength of the opinions that are held. In a large organisation, for example, it will often be difficult to involve a sufficient number of people in the sensing sessions to ensure that you are speaking to a genuinely representative sample, even if you have attempted to invite a broad cross-section of employees.

Even in a smaller organisation, because of the relative informality of the sensing sessions it may be difficult to aggregate the range of data produced. This group expressed more vehement views about an issue, but was this simply because they were a more outspoken group? That group raised the same issue but took a different perspective on it – how do we put the two sets of views together to draw a conclusion?

In general, we can assume that sensing, if effectively conducted, will successfully capture the great majority of significant issues in the organisation. However, it will often not provide us with a reliable picture of their *relative* importance or priority to the workforce as a whole. Because of this, if we wish to use the resulting data to inform decision-making or actions for change, it may often be useful to supplement the qualitatively focused sensing sessions with a more formal and quantitative employee survey.

Surveys and sensing

An employee survey provides us with a mechanism for testing and quantifying the data emerging from the sensing process. It enables us to test, with relative precision, what proportion of the workforce holds what views, and how strongly these views are held. Although it is possible to construct an employee survey without having first conducted some form of sensing or focus-group activity (based on one's existing knowledge of issues across the organisation), the two often provide usefully complementary information.

One approach, for example, is to hold sensing sessions both before and after a questionnaire-based survey. The initial sensing will identify the range of issues that are seen as important across the organisation. The survey then enables these to be tested, quantified and prioritised. However, the survey itself is a relatively blunt instrument: it allows quantification but cannot generally provide highly detailed insights into, for example, the reasons people have responded as they have (although, as we illustrate below, the survey can be constructed to provide some structured understanding of these kinds of issues). Because of this, it may be appropriate to conduct a further round of sensing once the survey results are available. These sessions can then be used to revisit the original issues in the context of the survey findings in order to gain a more detailed qualitative understanding of the views expressed.

Constructing the questionnaire

The purpose of the survey questionnaire, in essence, is to explore and validate your understanding of the issues evident in the organisation. The first step, therefore, is to identify the range of topics to be covered. This will depend partly on the nature and purpose of the survey but, in general, if the survey is genuinely to inform decisions or actions about change, it is preferable to limit the number of broad issues covered to no more than eight. If you try to cover more than this, the likelihood is that the data gathered will be superficial and unhelpful. The first task, therefore, is to prioritise those broad subject areas that seem most critical to the organisation.

Once you have identified the priority subject areas, the next step is to identify the range of questions that you wish to explore in each area. If the survey is being conducted following a sensing process, the sensing data will be invaluable in helping you to construct the questions.

It should be said at this point that, although most aspects of good questionnaire design are largely a matter of common sense (even if some consultants will encourage you to think otherwise), it is all too easy to design an ineffective or even potentially misleading questionnaire. For this reason, it may well be beneficial to seek expert support in this part of the process to ensure that the individual questions and the questionnaire as a whole reliably gather the information you are seeking. Key issues here include:

- relevance – does the question really address the issue you are interested in?

- precision – is the question sufficiently focused on the specific details you require? Will it be possible to interpret the answers with confidence?

- clarity – is the question easy to understand? Is it unambiguous?

Questions can be constructed in various formats. The most common approach in employee surveys, as in market research, is to use statements of opinion, attitude or behaviour followed by a rating scale, usually indicating the respondent's level of agreement with the statement – for example:

'My boss frequently gives me feedback on my performance'

Strongly Agree ☐   Agree ☐   Neither Agree Nor Disagree ☐   Disagree ☐   Strongly Disagree ☐

Many surveys are entirely constructed around these kinds of statement. The advantage of this approach is that it enables relatively precise analysis of specific attitudes or opinions about particular issues; in this case, we can measure the level of feeling about management feedback in the organisation. In addition, it is relatively easy to construct such statements from existing data. One approach, for example, is to extract suitable statements from the data gathered during the sensing session, ideally using the words actually uttered by participants. These kinds of statement-questions are also relatively easy to analyse, interpret and communicate, at least at a basic level. If the whole questionnaire is constructed in this way, for example, the findings can be presented very clearly and simply to managers and staff.

The disadvantage of this approach, however, is that it does not always allow us to interpret the detail of the response easily or to evaluate with any precision the differences between the various response categories. In the above case, for example, if I disagree that my boss frequently provides feedback, what precisely does this mean? Does my boss provide feedback on an *ad hoc* basis, sporadically, or not at all? And how frequent is frequently?

Some of these problems can be overcome by more careful design of the statements but, even so, this approach does not easily allow us to make links between questions or to assess the relative importance of different issues. If we have a series of statement-questions about a range of topics, the answers will tell us about respondents' attitudes to the individual issues, but they will not generally give us a sense of their relative significance.

For this reason, it is often helpful to vary the question formats so as to enable the questionnaire to collect different types of data. For example, it is possible to include some ranking questions that enable respondents to express their views about the relative importance of a range of issues. We might ask respondents to rank various aspects of organisational life – pay, terms and conditions, working environment, job satisfaction and so on – in terms of their perceived impact on the individual's desire to stay with the organisation. This may then highlight the fact that, say, although the working environment is poor, this is not a critical influence on people's decisions to stay or leave.

This kind of ranking question can also be helpful when there is concern that employees' answers may be unduly influenced by self-interest. For example, it is often difficult to ask questions about employee attitudes to their pay levels. We might all be tempted to claim that our pay is too low, even though objectively we recognise that we are remunerated fairly, if it seems that such a claim may influence the organisation to increase pay rates. However, if we are also asked to rank pay against other employment factors in terms of its importance to us, we are forced to declare our relative priorities. This then provides a context within which the responses on pay can be interpreted.

Funnelling

Putting the questions in context can be structured through a process that is sometimes known as 'funnelling', that is, drilling down from relatively wide-ranging questions to issues of precise detail. The broad process is illustrated in Figure 25:

Figure 25

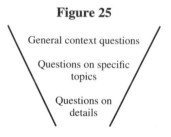

General context questions

Questions on specific topics

Questions on details

To take a simple example, we might begin the survey with a general ranking question, asking respondents to prioritise various aspects of organisation life – pay, working conditions, job satisfaction, training and so on. This question provides an overall context within which we can evaluate the responses on specific issues. So, for example, although employees may express dissatisfaction with a range of issues, we can judge which are the major priorities. If we have limited resources to invest in change, therefore, this will indicate where those resources are likely to be most usefully invested.

Once we have established the context, we can then begin to funnel down into the various topic areas. We might, for example, then include a range of questions on pay and reward, again funnelling down from context to detail. Our initial question might ask respondents to rank the importance of various aspects of reward – say, basic pay, bonuses, incentives, pensions or other benefits – again allowing us to evaluate their relative importance to respondents.

Finally, we can then investigate the detail of each aspect of pay. We might, for example, ask questions about the level and type of incentives used, the performance measures and assessment tools that underpin incentivisation, the perceived fairness of incentive arrangements, preferences for future incentives, and so on. This kind of approach can then be repeated across each aspect of the key issues under review.

By using the funnelling approach, an employee survey can enable the organisation to target its change activities with relative precision, in terms of their likely impact on employees. The survey findings will indicate which are the priority issues for employees, and – by funnelling down into the detail on each issue – highlight which elements need to be addressed first. If the survey is used effectively, it is possible to be relatively confident that the resulting changes will meet at least the perceived needs of the workforce.

Risks of sensing and surveys

Although sensing and survey techniques can be invaluable contributors to effective change, these tools do need to be handled with some care. First, it is important to remember that they provide only one perspective on the organisation. Although the views of employees will undoubtedly be highly important, they may not be paramount. While, for instance, employees may be dissatisfied with a particular arrangement or practice, there may nevertheless be sound business reasons for its continuation. In this case, it may well be appropriate to take some kind of action to address the employee concerns – perhaps by improving communication or finding a means of making the practice more attractive – but it may be inappropriate to make significant changes to the arrangement itself. In short, the findings should always be considered in the light of the wider business context.

Once the organisation has undertaken a sensing or survey exercise, it is critical that there is some form of response to the issues raised. One of the major risks of sensing or surveying is that simply because the exercise has been carried out, expectations will be raised. Employees will expect that some action will be taken as a result, and, if they have expressed any significant dissatisfactions, they will likewise expect these to be addressed.

To help manage these expectations, it is important that there is clear communication about the aims and purpose of the exercise, so that employees do not have any unrealistic expectations of the actions that might result. It is also helpful for the organisation to communicate in advance how it proposes to use the results of the exercise: how the data will be analysed and interpreted, what steps will be taken to turn the findings into action, what other factors will also need to be considered and so on.

Once the findings have been produced, the organisation ought to be seen to be responding to the issues that have emerged. This means, first of all, that the findings should be effectively communicated to the workforce. If the results are not communicated promptly, this will only raise suspicions that unsatisfactory results are being concealed. This in turn will serve only to intensify whatever dissatisfactions are already felt.

When the results have been published, the organisation then needs actively to respond. This does not mean that the organisation should act on every issue or concern raised, but it does mean that all issues should be explicitly addressed and that the organisation should fully explain any responses (positive or negative) that are made. If there is a decision not to make changes desired by employees, then the organisation needs to explain the factors that have been taken into account in making this decision. If employee expectations are disregarded without apparent good reason, the overall impact will generally be worse than if the sensing or survey had not taken place at all.

Above all, these techniques should not be used on a once-and-for-all basis. Sensing and survey techniques can be powerful mechanisms for informing the change process, but they should be a supplement to, rather than a replacement for, the normal communications channels. They provide a snapshot of potential change-issues at a point in time, but it is often helpful to continue the sensing process or to conduct periodic surveys as the change process continues, so that it is possible both to track the effects of change and to identify further, emerging requirements. In some organisations, these kinds of technique have become part of the fabric, accepted and understood by employees as part of the continuing process for dealing with change.

GUIDELINES

- *Spend* time discussing, presenting and gaining commitment to the sensing project

- *Ensure* sufficient time and resources to conduct the exercise

- *Build* confidence that the exercise will be more than a talking shop

- *Clarify* that attendance at the sensing group is mandatory

- *Decide* whether people will be selected from vertical or horizontal slices of the organisation

- *Determine* the mechanics of inviting people, meeting structure, questions to be asked, how information will be handled, location and so on

- *Set* limited objectives for each session

- *Promote* a relaxed, informal atmosphere in sensing sessions

- *Confirm* that named individual contributions are confidential and not disseminated

- *Offer* to switch off tape recorders if requested

- *Give* each sensing group warm-up issues to discuss

- *Send* written thanks to participants; confirm when the total exercise will end; state when action will start

- *Provide* participants with a brief summary of their own or the group's contribution

- *Analyse* both content and impressions from the sensing meetings

- *Present* findings to relevant power groups in the organisation

- *Use* employee surveys to test and quantify what proportion of the workforce holds what views, and how strongly these views are held

- *Limit* the number of broad topics to be covered by the survey to around six to eight – prioritise the issues that are most critical to the organisation

- *Ensure* that survey questions are relevant, precise and clear, and use experts to help design the questionnaire if you are in any doubt

- *Consider* varying the question formats, so as to enable the questionnaire to collect different types of data, and use 'funnelling' to drill down from wide-ranging contextual questions to issues of precise detail

- *Ensure*, to help managers manage expectations, clear communication about the aims and purpose of the survey

- *Ensure* also that the organisation communicates the results of the survey and is seen actively to respond to the findings.

18 Management by walking about

Robert McNamara, the former US Secretary of Defense, epitomised the analytical approach that has dominated much management thinking. During his period as a senior manager with the Ford Motor Company, he was convinced that a certain new model should show a particular level of fuel consumption. However, the results varied from one test to another.

The man in charge of the tests kept sending McNamara the figures, explaining that there were always variations in wind conditions, drivers and the cars themselves. McNamara was insistent. He had graphs and charts and he felt that the numbers simply must behave.

It was another Ford man who came to the rescue. He suggested to the man in charge of the tests: 'Why don't you do the testing and then, when it's done, I'll go in a corner and smooth the numbers a little?' The numbers were duly smoothed and brought to McNamara, who never went near the actual cars himself. McNamara beamed: the car was shown to be performing according to his numbers.

McNamara should have seen for himself what was happening. Because he disliked cars and was not too keen on meeting the people in the front line who were doing the actual work, he stayed tied to his desk, trying to control by numbers.

The importance of staying in close touch by walking around and seeing for yourself sounds so basic as to be hardly worth mentioning. Yet it is often neglected as a way of managing. Getting out and about is given all sorts of names: walking the shop floor, staying in touch, keeping a management profile, and even MBWA – Management by Walking (or Wandering) About. Contrary to an increasingly popular myth, Peters and Waterman were not the ones to discover it, although in their study of *Excellence* they drew attention to its importance, finding that it was a fundamental principle by which the highly successful Hewlett Packard computer firm operated. Nor is there any secret to it, although many managers seem reluctant either to do it or acknowledge its value.

At the tail-end of many a large organisational dinosaur, employees will often describe the lack of MBWA:

'The top brass? We never see them here.'
'Our head of department? Never comes near us.'
'Now you mention it, I've never even met the person in charge.'
'She visits all right, spends most of her time in the office with our supervisor.'
'Only time I've met the top boss was when I joined.'

These comments are rarer where managing change is valued and managers at all levels get out and about, staying in touch with what is, or is not, happening. No matter how senior you become, there is no substitute for MBWA.

In one highly profitable US confectionery firm, the head office appointed the managing director for the UK subsidiary at a salary far above the normal market rate. Before leaving for England for his new job, he received a message from head office: 'Good luck! Ask for help any time, but if there's a strike you're fired.' That MD soon acquired an obsession with staying in touch, leaving his desk, plunging into the factory, and visiting all the distribution points. He demanded such close contact with trade union representatives that he insisted on meeting them before they sought him out. By his walkabout approach he anticipated strikes, go-slows and overtime bans. He was so in touch that he could smell trouble coming.

Management by walking about is a question of seeing and talking to employees at all levels, learning what they are thinking, and tapping their ideas and enthusiasm. The larger the organisation, the more important this task becomes, especially for those in the rarefied atmosphere of the boardroom. A rather wider view of MBWA sees it as getting out among customers, suppliers, competitors, politicians – almost anyone outside the hierarchy.

Senior managers can spend their lives driving a desk, answering phone calls, handling colleagues' questions, ploughing through reading matter and being legitimately busy. Once in such a groove it requires a special effort to develop time for walkabouts.

Resist the tendency to become almost totally reliant on talking to your immediate peers. Although they have plenty in common with you and are usually sympathetic to your problems, such a narrow focus is apt to create management stagnation rather than the drive to promote change or learn whether agreed changes are actually happening.

How much in touch do you have to be? This becomes a dilemma as you ascend the corporate tree. Spend too little time walking about and you may be unpleasantly surprised by events. Spend too much time and you risk being forgotten by those at the centre. Staying in touch with all parts of your organisation develops your authority and prestige, and being well informed makes you valuable:

The bigger your job the more important it is to meet all levels of employees at their workplace.

Penetrating the structure

Managing by walking about helps reduce the stifling effects of the organisation's formal structure. Although the latter allows work to be organised and clarifies relationships between different employees, it also creates communication barriers. Walkabouts also reduce the isolation between senior and junior employees and between one section or unit and another, as you pass through sharing news, ideas and encouragement.

When there is serious trouble you need to be sure that you will be told about it and, if necessary, called in. Walkabouts guarantee that you are seldom far from some contact who can lead you to where your management input is required. From regular walkabouts you learn to sniff out the need for change. Seeing many different situations enables you to use your brain's computer-like ability to spot patterns and make new connections. You will often see opportunities that other people, apparently closer to the situation, have missed.

Walkabouts have a significant impact on employee morale and productivity. Evidence from the famous Hawthorne experiments, for example, suggested what managers do may be less important than the perception that they are trying to improve work situations.

By your presence at local workplaces you can actively encourage experiments, the generation of ideas and (perhaps most important) the habit of critical self-appraisal. This does not happen automatically, because much depends on your personal style and approach. A manager who arrives and immediately starts being highly critical would be wasting the power of MBWA. Once people who work for you know that you are genuinely interested in their contribution, you will seldom be short of vital information on ways to achieve better results.

A less obvious benefit from an MBWA style is that you are in a continuous learning situation. The stimulus should prevent you from becoming jaded or bored with your job. As many managers have discovered, walkabouts are fun.

Using MBWA you will find ways to reinforce change. For example, in one public-service agency, a senior manager launched a campaign to improve sickness rates. He visited several outposted staff locations with a vital piece of paper in his pocket. It contained a list of people who had just completed two years' continuous service without a day's sick leave, and he made a special point of personally congratulating them.

Behind many change efforts lies the need to introduce new value systems and influence norms. Using MBWA managers can talk to a wide range of employees about 'what we are trying to do', and explain that 'what really matters is . . .'.

How is it done?

'When I just wander round I'm not sure what to do or say' is how one anxious manager initially responded to the experience of building MBWA into his timetable. There are various ways of making it a rewarding experience. The most basic is being willing to listen, leaving space for people to talk to you, to share their feelings about what is happening. This is as important as your own message of change or new values. Stay quiet, smile and look interested and you will usually provoke a steady flow of news, views and useful information. In the US Sperry company, for example, the importance of listening has become a company obsession, and hundreds of managers have been trained to do it better. On walkabouts, keep your ratio of talking to listening at around 20:70 (see also Chapter 20 on Verbal Skills).

Focus your approach by selecting something highly specific to review during the MBWA. Just as scanning pages of print becomes easier if you are hunting for a particular fact or name, so with walkabouts a useful device is to seek specific kinds of information. This might include signs that employees are genuinely enjoying their work or, at worst, are not bored by it. For example, do employees seem to smile and catch your eye? Is there evidence that people are experimenting and testing out new ideas? One manager asked 'What's new?' so often that when he arrived people began beating him to it by asking *him* 'What's new?' Still, they realised that he valued change and wanted to hear about people trying new ways of doing things.

Develop a list of topic areas to check on regularly. A useful framework for formulating your search is the one presented in Box 34. The headings suggest various lines of enquiry to take during walkabouts.

If you work in a mainly hierarchical organisation, it makes sense to meet employees in groups or teams, sometimes with their supervisor present and occasionally alone. If you meet them without their immediate boss present, make it clear to all concerned that you will not be issuing any direct or indirect orders, which will avoid undermining the line manager's authority. You are there merely to encourage people to open up and talk about things that may sometimes be hard to share with their immediate supervisor. Request the meetings you need rather than arrive out of the blue. This will ensure that you do not disrupt other people's work too much except on a planned basis (see also Chapter 17 on Sensing and Surveys).

Box 34

Checkpoints for walkabouts

- *Leadership:* is there someone in this role at each level who keeps potential trouble-spots under control? How effective is this leadership: is it working well or badly?

- *Purposes:* employees must know what business they are in. Do people really understand the aims and values of the organisation?

- *Structure:* how is work organised? Is workload divided evenly?

- *Helpful mechanisms:* are there effective devices for enabling different parts of the organisation to work well together?

- *Relationships:* competing technologies and conflict between individuals must be managed well. Is this happening?

- *Incentives:* is there encouragement for doing all that needs to be done?

MBWA is a demanding experience. When you come face to face with those on the receiving end of change, they may unload on you some of the stresses they are experiencing. It is important therefore to:

Know your facts about the change and explain the benefits clearly.

Another peg on which to hang MBWA visits and a place to find pointers for discussions and enquiries is your organisation's philosophy or mission statement, with which everyone can readily identify. Bob Haas, the president and chief executive of Levi Strauss, the highly successful jeans and clothes concern, defined his company's philosophy as a set of goals relating to people, customers, the stores where clothes are sold and so on. For example, where people are concerned the philosophy states:

> Create a small company environment; establish a climate of openness; encourage risk taking; provide a safe, wholesome working environment that is stimulating, pleasant and supports maximum personal effectiveness.

Strauss executives on MBWA have a common view of what they expect to find and can test reality against expectations.

A possible drawback of MBWA is that people may see you as inspecting them – searching for things that they are doing wrong. You can avoid giving this impression by keeping your critical comments to a minimum and by not asking too many direct questions. Invite individuals to tell you what they are doing at that moment and to explain what they think about it. One manager, for example, who visited a work location stopped to look at some complicated forms that a clerk was completing. The clerk explained what she did and, while the manager stayed silent and showed interest, she proceeded to wonder aloud why the forms were not handled on a computer. The manager wondered too, and later installed a small computer system that released the clerk's time for more useful and interesting work.

Maintain a regular MBWA style by planning the visits in your diary several weeks or even months ahead. If you rely on snatching the occasional half-day you will soon be stuck behind a desk again. Tell people that you want to be invited when they have something new or interesting that they would like to share. This way the onus is not entirely on you to persist with MBWA. As a prompt, regularly review the check questions shown in Box 35. If you have junior managers or supervisors reporting to you, it is worth posing these questions to them too

Box 35

MBWA questions

- What work locations have been visited in the last two weeks?

- What was done to demonstrate or communicate the organisation's main mission(s) or central values?

- Apart from immediate working colleagues, to whom have you/I talked and what was learned?

- What recognition was offered for work done or successes?

- What action has been or will be taken as a result of the last visit?

- Will any successes or good practices be communicated elsewhere and, if so, how?

GUIDELINES

- *Change* your timetable so that walkabouts happen regularly

- *Focus* on specifics during the MBWA

- *Know* your facts about the change situation and be able to explain the benefits

- *Meet* employees in groups or teams, sometimes with their supervisor present and occasionally alone

- *Listen!* Keep your talking-to-hearing ratio at 20:70

- *Avoid* criticism; if you must criticise, do it simply

- *Enquire* what individuals are doing right now and encourage them to explain what they think about it

- *Let* people know that you want to be asked to visit when they have something new, interesting or particular problems they would like to share

- *Avoid* too many direct questions

- *Look* for activities to praise

- *Seek* news of activities designed to increase productivity, develop communications, do things better and so on

- *Enquire* about failures and show that responsible attempts to improve things will be encouraged

- *Avoid* giving orders directly to subordinates of managers below you

- *Never* reprimand someone in front of other people.

19   Team-building

When Malcolm Payne became responsible for a newly formed division in a large international travel agency, he found many of the services provided were of low quality and unco-ordinated, and staff morale was poor. His major change action was a restructuring, which he introduced in the first few months. This clarified lines of accountability, reduced spans of control and created new lines of communication.

After meeting all the managers for whom he was responsible, Malcolm realised that to restructure effectively required more than just arranging the pieces of the organisational jigsaw. There had to be new ways of working; new formal relationships had to be reinforced; and, above all, people had to learn to work together in a more concerted way. What was needed was team-building.

All managers and supervisors met for a day to review how to use teamwork in order to build on the changes already made. Obstacles to effective teams were reviewed and ways of eliminating them identified. The various teams were encouraged to take one or more days away from the workplace to review their effectiveness and goals in relation to the division's overall objectives. Senior managers were available to help at the sessions, and in certain teams that required a considerable amount of help an outside organisational consultant was used.

These team sessions reduced hidden resentment about the recent reorganisation and began harnessing people's creative energies. Teams were asked to set specific aims for the coming months, and in this way members began experiencing shared goals. Regular team-building sessions became a legitimate activity in which managers and staff could invest their time. From these stemmed many of the improvements envisaged at the start of the reorganisation.

Organisations totally committed to coping with change realise the importance of teamwork. They convert the negative backbiting behaviour usually associated with 'politics' into something positive by emphasising teamwork. Looking at Morgan Bank, Bankers Trust, IBM and Olivetti in Italy, consultant Robert Waterman Jr asked: 'Where is the frenzy? The fervour? The angst? Don't these people watch television and know that life is supposed to be frantic? . . How can they be so calm yet do so well in today's "fast paced, split-second, rate-of-change-was-never-greater" world? The answer is teamwork, which starts at the top.'

Effective teamwork seldom happens by chance or luck. It stems from sound leadership and the use of principles that any change-minded manager can use.

Harder than it looks

There is an important distinction between working in teams and team-building. Although many managers are responsible for teams, they are not always committed to any investment in team-building. While supporting the idea of teams, some people assume that the team-building process occurs naturally. It can do, particularly if the group is facing intense pressure or stress. But actively building a team offers a more systematic way of speeding up the cohesion of the group, which can otherwise take months or years to achieve.

As a way of achieving organisational change team-building is increasingly being given a high priority. In contrast, some people believe that it is the efforts of individuals that really count in making things happen. Teams may also be judged to be irrelevant for dealing with many of the major issues currently concerning the organisation, which itself may not see organisational change as a key issue.

For anyone committed to team-building as a way of achieving change it can be frustrating that not everyone embraces this approach. When pressed by an enthusiastic colleague to pursue team-building, one manager retorted: 'You're proselytising. Well, it's not a sect that I want to join.' His reaction reflects how many people feel when faced with team-building enthusiasts. If a group of people must work together regularly, it does not automatically follow that they should function like a team with common goals, mutual respect and shared values.

Another objection to team-building as a way of achieving organisational change is that it simply takes too long. However, most major worthwhile organisational changes also take a long time, so that team-building is seldom a waste of time.

Organisations that cope well with change are usually those where the importance of relationships between groups and individuals is acknowledged and there is an emphasis on interdependence and shared responsibility. This requires an openness, a willingness to confront issues and individuals, and a recognition that the efforts of a group can often be more effective than the same number of people working separately. In handling change, therefore, managers need skills that encourage the interdisciplinary approach, particularly for tackling difficult or complex situations such as creating a corporate strategy.

Influencing how groups interact with each other has been widely used as a way both to generate and to respond to change. In recent years there has also been a growing awareness of the importance of helping individuals transcend their team role in the interest of developing themselves and the enterprise. Team-building is thus no panacea but, when it is used selectively, it can:

- create a climate of social support for a particular change

- open up the communication processes

- encourage creative problem-solving

- obtain commitment to decisions

- assist in achieving individual and organisational goals

- foster interdependence and group effort.

Making a start

How do you build a successful, change-minded team? The first step is to identify the group of people who you think should be working as a team. Try defining:

Why should this group of people work as a team?

To do this, answer the questions shown in Box 36. The answers can usefully involve the group of people themselves in thinking about the two main issues:

Are we a team?

Should we work at becoming a (better) team?

To start team-building, you may wish to use a training specialist or a consultant with relevant experience. Alternatively, you can lead the team-building yourself using do-it-yourself guides such as those listed in the further reading section at the end of this book. You may also decide that you want some training on team-building methods; there are many courses available on this subject.

Whoever organises the process should see that the group takes time away from daily work pressures to concentrate on specific team-building tasks. These may be a mixture of working on issues facing the group and particularly techniques that promote teamwork.

Box 36

Deciding if a group is a team

- Do people have more things in common than differences – YES/NO

- Are there complex issues which are better tackled using many people's ideas and skills – YES/NO

- Can someone be identified as a team leader, manager or 'chairman' with a role to promote teamwork – YES/NO

- Are the individuals willing to work together more closely – YES/NO

- Is it practical in terms of time, travel distances and other constraints for this group to meet regularly to work both formally as a team and on the process of team building – YES/NO

If the answer is NO to any of these questions, team building is likely to be inappropriate.

Forcing the group to do something exceptionally challenging is another, somewhat controversial, way of speeding up the team-building process. The latter must involve activities designed to help the individuals get to know each other better, find out each other's strengths and weaknesses, and learn to trust each other. One British managing director took his entire top team, including their wives, to climb the highest mountain in Central Africa. This proved a life-changing experience for all concerned, and they returned to form a work group with tremendous cohesion and trust.

Team roles

Are you a shaper or a company worker? Or is finishing your preference? Perhaps you see yourself mainly as a team worker or someone who likes monitoring and evaluating? If none of these, how about being chairman? Roles like these make or break a management team. Omit one, and the team may never rise above the average.

One of the most thorough investigations undertaken to unravel why management teams succeed or fail was by Meredith Belbin, who studied hundreds of teams and thousands of managers. His results are often used to improve a team's functioning. People play eight main roles in management teams. Each has some positive features and some weaknesses. Successful teams are a mixture of people whose skills complement each other (see Box 37).

Belbin had enviable opportunities to create entirely new teams, experimenting until he found the right recipe. Few managers in real life, even those determined to shake up the entire organisation, have the chance to start with a blank sheet and devise the ideal team. Most managers inherit their teams, or part of them, and must use the available skills to obtain the best results.

To prepare for looking at team roles, the members must first read Belbin's book on *Team Management*, or a lengthy summary of it. Each person then completes a simple questionnaire from which is produced a team and an individual profile. These show the leanings each person has towards the eight roles and what kind of mix of roles exist in the team as a whole.

As an individual, you learn your role preferences, which can be compared with those of your colleagues. The profiles provide the starting-point for considering how the team can begin functioning better. They can also uncover why the team occasionally wastes time through handling some tasks inefficiently.

Although individuals may emerge as strong in a particular role, this does not mean that they must always play that role. They may be only slightly less powerful in another role that is badly needed in the particular team. The assumption behind the role mixture is that successful teams contain a sufficient variety of people for all eight roles to be represented. The team should accept the importance of each role as contributing towards collective success. Another assumption is that people can switch roles.

Superficially, Shaper and Chairman seem to be the prestige roles, the ones for which highly competitive members of the team may fight. In practice, however, these roles are successful only in combination with others. For instance, a team with too many Shapers may undervalue the person who regularly reminds the team that it must complete its task – Completer/Finisher. Similarly, a team full of aspiring Chairmen may spend time fighting for the leadership while devaluing someone who is good at providing information on which the team can make choices – Resources Investigator.

Once the team realises how its profile affects performance, it becomes easier to change the situation. For example, a public-services agency team working on the Belbin analysis found that it was short of Finishers. The team tended to assume that once a decision was made, action would automatically happen. Follow-through often failed to materialise. Using role analysis, the team revised how it dealt with decisions. As each new decision was made it was written on a large flipchart and a name was assigned as responsible for the next steps. The flipchart became the team's action minutes.

Using role analysis, a team in one organisation improved its choice of who to represent it at other meetings. If they wanted to stir things up

Box 37

Useful people to have in teams

Team worker	Typical features	Positive qualities	Allowable weaknesses
Company Worker	Conservative, dutiful, predictable	Organising ability, practical common sense, hard-working, self-disciplined	Lack of flexibility, unresponsiveness to unproven ideas
Chairman	Calm, self-confident, controlled	A capacity for treating and welcoming all potential contributors on their merits and without prejudice. A strong sense of objectives	No more than ordinary in terms of intellect or creative ability
Shaper	Highly strung, outgoing, dynamic	Drive and a readiness to challenge inertia, ineffectiveness, complacency or self-deception	Prone to provocation, irritation and impatience
Plant	Individualistic, serious-minded, unorthodox	Genius, imagination, intellect, knowledge	Up in the clouds, inclined to disregard practical details or protocol
Resources Investigator	Extrovert, enthusiastic, curious, communicative	A capacity for contacting people and exploring anything new. An ability to respond to challenge	Liable to lose interest once the initial fascination has passed
Monitor – Evaluator	Sober, unemotional, prudent	Judgement, discretion, hard-headedness	Lacks inspiration or the ability to motivate others
Teamworker	Socially oriented, rather mild, sensitive	An ability to respond to people and to situations, and to promote team spirit	Indecisiveness at moments of crisis
Completer/ Finisher	Painstaking, orderly, conscientious, anxious	A capacity for follow-through. Perfectionism	A tendency to worry about small things. A reluctance to 'let go'

Source: Team Management: Why management teams succeed or fail, Belbin, J, London, Heinemann, 1981

and promote action, they would send a Shaper, or even a Plant. If there was a need for someone to see through a detailed piece of work, maintaining good relations with everyone and being highly diplomatic, then it would send a Team or Company Worker.

Role analysis highlights the opportunity for team members to play several roles, particularly if there are only a few members. Also, if several people are competing, perhaps unconsciously, for the chairmanship role, the power struggle may leave everyone feeling drained and demoralised. Using role analysis, some members may see the value of modifying their natural chairmanship inclinations so that the team becomes more successful.

Role analysis has proved useful in many organisations, from ICI's paint division to social services departments, in focusing the team-building effort. However, it is merely one approach among many.

Responsibility-charting

It is sometimes helpful to clarify responsibilities within the organisation. This can be particularly important when pursuing major change goals. Suppose, for example, a senior management team in a large retail chain of shops decides to unlock the value of the company's many high-street properties. The team may assign different tasks to its members who, individually or in groups, implement the decision. Other people may also take part, contributing to the plan without necessarily being responsible for the work itself. What starts as a straightforward idea becomes increasingly complex, involving many people. Clarifying accountability may be essential if the team and the change effort are to succeed. Responsibility-charting helps obtain such clarification. Although initially appearing cumbersome it has been widely used to:

- *identify* who will do what on new decisions

- *show* why decisions already taken have not been performed as intended

- *improve* the way in which the team itself functions.

Responsibility-charting requires a systematic approach and a willingness to debate vigorously those issues that it highlights. Although it can be useful to have someone outside the team to lead the charting exercise, it is not essential, and managers can use it with a bit of practice.

The first step is to list all the types of decisions to be made. These are added down one side of a grid. Along the top is shown all the actors involved in the work as a whole (see Figure 25).

Figure 25

Resonsibility chart

	R	– Responsibility (initiates)
	A-V	– Approval (right to veto)
	S	– Support (put resources against)
	I	– Inform (to be informed)

Actors → Decision ↓												

Source: Organizational Transactions: Managing complex change, Richard Beckhard and Reuben T. Harris, 1977, Reading, MA. Addison-Wesley, Figure 6.1

Charting proceeds by taking each decision and assigning one of four types of behaviour to each of the actors:

- *Responsibility (R)* – for initiating action to ensure that the decision is carried out. For example, it might be the managing director's responsibility to initiate an annual review of the organisation's performance.

- *Approval or right to veto (A-V)* – a decision. For example, a manager may have the right to approve or veto whether someone takes part in a project initiated by someone else.

- *Support (S)* – provide logistical support and resources for the particular decision. For example, an accountant might be asked for information on some aspect of an agreed decision yet have no right to initiate action, exercise approval or veto it.

- *Inform (I)* – must be kept informed, with no right to influence the decision directly. For example, a training manager may have the right to be kept informed about new developments without a right to influence whether they proceed.

The work group debates each decision or action and against each person assigns a responsibility using the appropriate letters – R, A-V, S, and I – which are added to the grid. Anyone not participating at all in the decision is shown with a simple dash (-).

Assigning to each decision or task an appropriate responsibility and person is revealing, though time-consuming. Intense debate may finally reveal that someone initially given a veto power is the real decision-maker. New understandings from charting responsibilities can ensure that required changes really do occur.

The system is most effective when the team insists on assigning responsibility for particular items to only one person, even though several may be needed to implement it. Similarly, on any one decision or task, only a few people should be granted the Approval-Veto function, otherwise it will slow down or prevent implementation. Equally, by giving one person the right to approve or veto most decisions there is a danger of creating bottlenecks or power blockages.

The Support function should be fully discussed, because the person who acquires this has a crucial role using resources to help the person ultimately responsible for the overall action.

Responsibility-charting can be fun to do and bring to light unexpected perspectives on the change effort. Like Circles of Influence (see Chapter 6 on Power and Influence), it makes work on change more systematic by stimulating new ways of tackling what seem immovable blockages.

GUIDELINES

- *Gain* support for the change effort through systematic team-building

- *Don't* try to treat every work group as a formal team

- *Discover* whether there are sound reasons for a group of people to work as a team

- *Consider* who will lead the team-building effort

- *Ensure* that the group has time away from daily work-pressures to concentrate on team-building

- *Use* existing team problems and tested methods for the team-building effort

- *Analyse* which role each team member should play, and the mix of roles within the team

- *Consider* using responsibility-charting to clarify the involvement of people in different decisions and actions.

20 Verbal skills

Are you convincing and persuasive? How do you rate your verbal skills? To affect change in your organisation, good conversation skills are essential. There tends to be a direct relationship between a person's range of vocabulary and his or her likely status, power and prestige.

The more successful people are at ascending the management hierarchy, the better they usually are at communicating in words and phrases. Although we usually equate communication with words and sounds, we must never forget that these are always alongside (and sometimes replaced by) non-verbal messages. In fact, of the messages that human beings give each other, non-verbal messages predominate.

Figure 26

Human messages:
the cues and signals we give

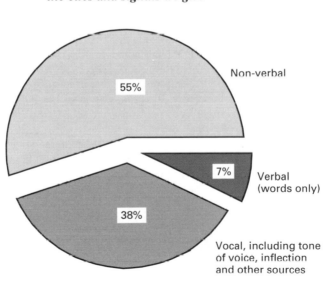

221

Some other research findings about verbal skills for managers are shown in Box 38.

Box 38

Some research findings on verbal skills

- The person who participates most actively in group activities where no one has been appointed or elected to lead is most likely to emerge as leader

- Oral communication abilities have been rated highest as a needed supervisory skill

- Industrial supervisors have reported that they most wanted to learn 'how to sell ideas to my superior'

- When in a group, high-status people do not perceive any loss of influence if they change their opinions several times during a discussion

- More rapid promotion of managers is related to interpersonal competence

- The sheer quantity or percentage of time in interaction and working with others seems to contribute to one's success as a leader

- There is a direct relationship between status, power and prestige and a person's range of vocabulary

---

Influencing change involves persuading others to accept new ideas and a different *status quo*. Verbal skills and an understanding of non-verbal cues are important for obtaining that acceptance. Verbal skills include those shown in Box 39. Rate yourself from one to five on how effective you are at each of these 20 skills. Better still, ask a colleague who knows you well to rate you. Add up your scores and, if you obtain a score of less than 85, read on!

Most talking is impromptu and open to misunderstandings. Words are misheard, intonations misinterpreted, something unintended is conveyed. For instance, if you receive a note from the trade union asking what you are going to do about a pay anomaly, there is time to analyse it and send a considered response. Faced with the same question in a management–union meeting and under pressure to respond, you may betray your ignorance or become committed to unnecessary action.

Managers are generally better at talking than listening. Yet the problems associated with change frequently stem from too little listening. It is dangerous to assume that those on the receiving end usually understand us – mostly they are failing to understand. Research into listening by the Sperry Company found success rates of communication of only 25 per cent. In other words, three-quarters of communications are not really understood.

Box 39

Verbal skills managers need

- Listen actively
- Negotiate
- Say no
- Deal with personal criticism
- Present proposals and sell ideas
- Disagree without being aggressive or rude
- Offer praise
- Criticise constructively
- Contribute to meetings
- Make a formal speech in front of strangers
- Argue logically
- Sound committed
- Summarise accurately what others have said
- Avoid interrupting
- Chair meetings
- Redefine 'problems' as 'opportunities'
- Obtain information that people are trying to conceal
- Use questions without sounding inquisitorial
- State complicated things simply
- Handle differences of opinion

Courses on negotiating, chairing meetings, making presentations, giving a speech and so on all teach aspects of verbal skills. Such skills make you a better all-round manager and are essential in any change effort that you lead. Some verbal skills can be learned from reading and then practising in situations where making mistakes does not matter. Some basics are covered in the rest of this chapter.

Non-verbals

Alongside verbal interaction is the vast amount of non-verbal communication made with eyes, heads, limbs and other bodily gestures. Although the verbal channel conveys mainly information, the non-verbal channel negotiates interpersonal attitudes and, in some cases, is a direct substitute for a verbal message.

Understanding people by looking at them and adapting your verbal response appropriately is an art with a long history of folklore and half-truth. The main lesson from research is:

A single non-verbal gesture is seldom enough from which to draw conclusions.

Watch for several linked gestures rather than a single event. Once you start noticing them you will begin using them to tailor your everyday verbal approach. For instance, what would you conclude if your boss listens with one hand on his cheek, index finger pointing upwards, another finger covering his mouth and the thumb supporting the chin, and his legs crossed? Studies of non-verbal cues suggest that these combined signals reveal: 'I don't like what you are saying and I disagree with you.'

You can adapt your verbal response by translating the unspoken language. If you notice that someone adopts your own general bodily posture, for example, such as leaning forward or sitting with hands in a like manner, it can signal that you are succeeding in your persuasion efforts.

Most managers know something about eye movement and contact and how it encourages or deters talking. It also signals 'I'm glad to see you' or 'I know that you are here.' For instance, a senior manager may pass through to his own room giving a nod, half smile or wave, matched with a brief moment of eye contact to recognise and acknowledge each person in the outer office.

Verbal skills thus include knowing about active listening, body language, use of personal space, eye contact and so on. Freud concluded that 'no mortal can keep a secret. If his lips are silent he chatters with his finger tips; betrayal oozes out of him at every pore.'

Conflict resolution

Challenging the *status quo* often causes conflict. To handle change well, managers need the verbal skills to deal with conflict. These involve discussions in which you separate:

- problems from solutions

- facts from opinions

- feelings from logical reasoning.

A framework for tackling conflict can be helpful, particularly if you are the kind of person who finds conflict unpleasant. The main conflict-management steps are shown in Box 40.

Box 40

The steps for managing conflict

1 CONFRONT the conflict – acknowledge to yourself that a conflict exists; communicate to the other party that there is a conflict; assert positively your wants, wishes and preferences

2 UNDERSTAND the other person's position – listen; give feedback and restate his or her position to show you understand; use 'I' statements rather than 'you' blame/language

3 DEFINE the problem(s) – try to reach a mutually acceptable definition of the problem; avoid a combatative approach at this stage; acknowledge your strengths and vulnerabilities; be prepared to change if necessary; be honest

4 SEARCH for and evaluate alternative solutions – collaborate to obtain a mutually acceptable solution; separate creating alternatives from evaluating them; solve the most manageable problems first; ask 'Which solution looks best?' not 'Which do I prefer?'

5 AGREE on and implement the best solution(s) – treat the agreement like a contract, seek great clarity and specificity; state who will do what, by when etc

Some of the blocks to sorting out conflict may also stem directly from a manager's lack of verbal skills, such as those shown in Box 41.

Questions

Senior managers generally pride themselves on their ability to ask the right questions. Questions steer conversation and direct interactions. They can indeed be powerful and should be used sparingly. Because most interactions contain some kind of questioning, you should become familiar with the main types of questions shown in Box 42.

Asking a question is less effective if the person is unsure why you are asking it. For example, if your boss asks 'Where were you yesterday?', it could be followed by either 'because I wanted to invite you to lunch' or 'because I couldn't find you and had to deal with a problem that was your responsiblity'. Questions thus spring from a variety of directions or motives, and if those on the receiving end are unsure about these, they may be defensive, guarded or aggressive. What happens when you ask one question is even worse when a barrage of questions is launched. Like trouble, questions seldom come singly, and escalate with each succeeding answer.

Questions can work well when you explain their purpose. If you are

Box 41

Blocks to resolving conflicts

- WRONG LANGUAGE – combatative rather than collaborative verbal and non-verbal communications

- NOT CONFRONTING – failing to acknowledge differences; not raising issues; raising them in an aggressive way and creating defensiveness

- POOR TIMING – you talk of conflict when either you or they are not ready to acknowledge or handle it

- EXCESS TALKING – not listening to the other's point of view; being too ready to criticise; leaving the other person no space to express feelings

- MISUSE OF LANGUAGE – 'you-blame' rather than 'I' statements; emotive words like 'you idiot', 'that's crazy' or other put downs; repeating your views too much and appearing domineering

- VOCAL EXCESSES – dominating with a loud voice; frightening with a shrill voice; chilling with a cold voice

- LACK OF OPENNESS – you fail to state the real reason for the conflict; you lie; you suppress information particularly if it is unfavourable to your case; not admitting negative or positive feelings you have for the other party

- POOR ANGER CONTROL – you own or other people's

unwilling to explain why you need to know something, then your communications with others will not be considered open or helpful. If delivered effectively, so that the other person understands why you are asking them, questions:

Offer scope to provide general information
or
elicit specific answers.

The first of these is a divergent approach, opening up opportunties for communication. Divergent-type questions steer the conversation away from a single response or specific reply. If you want to explore a situation, discover what people are thinking, develop new ideas, then a divergent approach using open-ended questions, redefining questions and ones that pose no threat are the best way of achieving results.

Box 42

Questions that managers ask

- CLOSED QUESTIONS – seek precise, brief information: 'Do you have a degree?'; 'What is the sales turnover?'; 'Have you met Mr Jones?'

- OPEN-ENDED QUESTIONS – encourage the other person to feel there are no conversational boundaries: 'How are things going?'; 'What's it like working here?'

- DIRECT QUESTIONS – demand more information than simple closed questions because they assert your authority and right to know something: 'Why did that happen?'; 'Who is involved in this?'; 'What authority did you have to overspend?'

- INDIRECT QUESTIONS – gain information obliquely: 'When are you going to leave the company?' may be less effective than 'What are your personal career plans over the next few years?'; or 'Do you have a contingency plan?' may be less effective than, 'How would we cope in an emergency?'

- HYPERBOLIC QUESTIONS – provoke the other person, perhaps to a denial, an admission or to offer some refutation: 'Is it true that you're going broke?' 'Heavens no! But I do admit that we're having a problem with debtor accounts.'

- REDEFINING QUESTIONS – restate a problem or a situation to help break an impasse or deal with conflict: 'Would you agree that another way of looking at it is . . .?'

- RHETORICAL QUESTIONS – make statements in a way that indicate that no answer is required, either because it is obvious or not expected: 'If that is the annual loss, what hope is there for the firm's survival?'; 'Surely we shouldn't just sit and do nothing about it?'

- LEADING QUESTIONS – suggest what the answer should be: 'Do you accept that you were negligent?'; 'Would you agree that . . .?'

The second approach is a convergent one in which questions narrow down answers towards a single target area. You are less interested in exploration and more concerned with gaining hard information quickly. Closed, direct and leading questions all tend to steer the conversation into relatively narrow channels.

Next time you ask a question, think about whether you are opening up or closing down a range of possibilities for an answer.

If you enjoy using questions, use them sparingly and avoid a gun-slinger style of delivery.

Assertiveness

Assertiveness is when you insist that your views, feelings and needs are considered. This implies standing up for your rights and handling other people's undesirable behaviour.

A right is something to which you are entitled. In any situation you have rights. For instance, a manager has the right to expect and receive typing of the required standard and to show mistakes to the typist. The typist has the right to have these mistakes mentioned in a reasonable manner without being humiliated or feeling under personal attack. Asserting your rights and respecting the rights of others are inextricably linked with achieving change.

To influence change, managers must be seen as positive and constructive people who are meeting both their own needs and those of other people in the organisation. Being positive and constructive, often in the face of resistance and other negative factors, means being assertive.

Assertiveness is essential because it encourages assertion in others, so that people are more likely to continue working with, rather than against you. Considerable evidence exists to show that lack of assertiveness and aggression stem from low self-esteem (what you think about yourself and how you evaluate your worth as a person).

When you consider yourself to be competent, significant, likeable and successful, you have high self-esteem. With low self-esteem you will be anxious and uncertain, and you will communicate this in the way you talk and behave, making it harder to convince others about the need for change.

Assertion means also standing up for your own rights, needs and beliefs without violating those of other people. People behaving assertively do the kind of things shown in Box 43. Next time you listen to a conversation at work, try classifying it in terms of whether it is assertive, non-assertive or aggressive. As with recognising and interpreting non-verbal cues, this requires practice. Raising your own personal consciousness about what is happening will improve your effectiveness.

When you are introducing change, you must constantly ask people for help and be competent at handling situations in which people disagree, resist and generally express doubts about what is being proposed. Thus, two crucial skills are making requests and disagreeing without aggression.

By making requests assertively, you seek help in a way that makes people want to assist, without feeling that they have no choice. Likewise, you must cope with the many situations in which there is some disagreement about what should be done. Box 44 offers hints on making requests and disagreeing without aggression.

Box 43

Assertive people tend to

- USE 'I' statements such as 'I think . . .' 'I want . . .' 'I feel . . .'

- MAKE brief statements, to the point, not rambling ones

- DISTINGUISH between fact and opinion

- OFFER suggestions without heavily loaded advice': 'How about tackling it this way . . . ?'; 'Have you tried . . . ?'; 'Would it be possible to . . . ?'

- POSE constructive criticism, stating *facts* about people's action, not attacking them as people

- DISCOVER thoughts, opinions and wants of others through questions

- SEEK solutions, ways of getting round problems: 'Is there some way we could . . . ?'; 'Maybe if we tried . . . ?'; 'Another way might be . . .'

Box 44

Hints on making requests and disagreeing without aggression

Making requests	*Disagreeing without aggression*
NEVER apologise for seeking help	STATE clearly that you disagree
BE direct	EXPRESS doubts constructively
KEEP it short	USE 'I' statements
DON'T try to justify yourself	CHANGE your opinion in the light of
GIVE a reason for your request	new information
NEVER sell the request with flattery	GIVE reasons for your disagreement
or promises	SAY exactly what you disagree with
AVOID playing on people's friend-	RECOGNISE other people's point of
ship or good nature	view
DON'T take a refusal personally	
RESPECT the other person's right to	
say no	

These are just some of the assertiveness techniques that you can adopt.

Feedback

Feedback is another easily acquired verbal skill and a powerful tool during the change effort as you seek to discover how to persuade people to do things and uncover reasons for resistance. Helpful feedback includes the kinds shown in Box 45.

Box 45

Helpful feedback is
• descriptive, not evaluative
• specific, not general
• relevant to the self-perceived needs of the receiver
• desired by the receiver, not imposed
• timely and in context
• usable, concerned with things over which the receiver has some control

Top 10 hints

Charles Margerison, Professor of Management at the University of Queensland, has worked with many managers to improve their verbal skills. He offers a useful 10-point guide on conversational control:

- *Listen for the cues and clues* – key words and phrases indicating points of interest or concern; don't change the topic of conversation when people use 'I', 'me' or 'my' and adjectives showing they are annoyed, worried, happy and so on.

- *Learn to move from being problem-centred to solution-centred and back again* – stay in the problem-centred area until you know enough about causes.

- *Manage your conversational time* – prevent conversations from becoming fixated with one time-dimension (such as the past); deal with the present and the future.

- *Take a personal interest in permissions and territory* – permission is about seeking agreement to discuss certain matters, directly or indirectly: 'I'd like to talk to you about this note you wrote to me.' Territory is when people claim something for their own: 'I'm not prepared to discuss that'; 'I'm sorry, these minutes only go to members of the project team.'

- *Seek the win/win option as the priority* – the best conversations are those in which both participants emerge winners, having gained something.

- *Manage both facts and opinions* – never allow one to dominate at the expense of the other; where you have many opinions, seek facts; if you have a lot of facts, seek opinions.

- *Convert the verbals to the visuals* – give people an opportunity to see and hear by presenting information visually.

- *Give accurate summaries, understand before you judge* – summarise regularly and accurately to gain agreement.

- *Assert yourself* – stand up for what you want without being aggressive; understand and recognise what the other person has said, and then be positive about putting forward what you want.

- *Emphasise the positives* – watch out for the negative tendencies in your conversations; get people thinking about 'how to' rather than 'how not to'.

These points are explained in more detail in Margerison's book on *Conversational Skills for Managers* (see References and Further Reading at the end of this book).

Finally, taking the last of these hints a bit further, have you tried measuring your 'but quotient (BQ)'? Someone with an open mind tends to have a BQ close to zero. The word *but* is a truly powerful negator. Its negative effect is far greater than you intend, on others and yourself. Reduce your BQ by using the word *and* without making it sound like *but*!

GUIDELINES

- *Watch* non-verbal behaviour; look for linked gestures; never rely on just one to interpret meaning

- *Handle* conflict by:
  - separating problems from solutions, facts from opinions and logical reasoning from feelings
  - confronting it
  - understanding the other person's position
  - defining the problem(s)
  - looking for, evaluating and implementing the best solution(s)

- *Use* questions sparingly

- *Ask* questions in a non-threatening way by explaining why you are asking them

- *Assert* yourself by standing up for your rights and dealing with others' undesirable behaviours

- *Make* requests and disagree without aggression

- *Use* the Margerison 10-point guide for conversational control

- *Minimise* your '*but* quotient'.

References and further reading

Chapter 1 – Models

WHYTE W F. 'Models for building and changing organisations', in *The Management of Change and Conflict* by Thomas M J and Bennis W G, London, Penguin, 1972, pp 227–238

TICHEY N. 'The essentials of strategic change management'. *Journal of Business Strategy*, spring 1983

LIMERICK D *and* CUNNINGHAM B. 'Management development: the fourth blueprint'. *Journal of Management Development*, Volume 6, No 1, 1987

HUCZYNSKI H. *Encyclopedia of Organizational Change Methods*. Aldershot, Gower Publishing Company, 1987, pp 5–15

Chapter 2 – Leadership

HAMPDEN-TURNER C *and* TROMPENAARS F. *The Seven Cultures of Capitalism*. London, Piatkus, 1994

HESSELBEIN F, GOLDSMITH M *and* BECKHARD R (eds). *The Leader of the Future*. New York, Jossey-Bass, 1996

SAYLES L. *Leadership, What Effective Managers Really Do and How They Do It*. Maidenhead, McGraw-Hill, 1979

STOGDILL'S *Handbook of Leadership*, ed. Bass B M, Free Press, 1981

NICHOLLS J R. 'A new approach to situational leadership', *Leadership and Organization Development Journal*, Vol 6, 1985

TICHEY N *and* DEVANNA M A. *The Transformational Leader*. Chichester, John Wiley, 1986

Chapter 3 – Vision and values

CAMPBELL A *and* TAWADAY K. *Mission and Business Philosophy*. Oxford, Heinemann, 1990

COLLINS J C *and* PORRAS J I. *Built to Last*. London, Century Ltd, 1994

TICHEY N *and* DEVANNA M A. 'Creating a motivating vision', in *The Transformational Leader*, Chichester, John Wiley, 1986, pp 90–147

BLOCK P. *The Empowered Manager: Positive political skills at work*. New York, Jossey-Bass, 1987, pp 99–129

PLANT R. *Managing Change and Making it Stick*. London, Fontana, 1987, pp 73–86

SCULLEY J. *Odyssey*. London, William Collins, 1987, pp 323–328

PETERS T. *Thriving on Chaos*. London, Macmillan, 1988, p 398–408

WILLIAMS A, DOBSON P *and* WALTERS M. *Changing Culture: New organisational approaches*. 2nd edn. London, Institute of Personnel and Development, 1993

Chapter 4 – Commitment

MARTIN P and NICHOLS J. *Creating a Committed Workforce*. London, Institute of Personnel Management, 1987

TICHEY N and DEVANNA M A. 'Mobilising Commitment', in *The Transformational Leader*. Chichester, John Wiley, 1986, pp 149–182

WATERMAN R Jr. *The Renewal Factor*. Bantam Press, 1988, pp 293–312

Chapter 5 – Communication

JACKSON P C. *Corporate Communication for Managers*. London, Pitman, 1987

REDDING C W. *The Corporate Manager's Guide to Better Communication*. New York, Scott Foresman, 1984

SCOTT B. *The Skills of Communication*. London, Gower, 1986

Chapter 6 – Power and influence

KOTTER J. *Power in Management*. AMACON, 1979

WATERMAN R Jnr. *The Renewal Factor*. London, Bantam Press, 1988, pp 199–212

Chapter 7 – Resistance to change

HULTMAN K. *The Path of Least Resistance*. Texas, Learning Concepts, 1979

TICHEY N *and* DEVANNA M A. *The Transformational Leader*. Chichester, John Wiley, 1986, pp 59–86

Chapter 8 – Planning strategic change

QUINN J. 'Strategic change: logical incrementalism', *Sloan Management Review*, Vol 20, No 1, 1978

KANTER R. *The Change Masters*. London, Allen and Unwin, 1984, pp 294–296

SCULLEY J. *Odyssey*. London, William Collins, 1987, pp 292–297

PUMPIN C. *The Essence of Corporate Strategy*. Aldershot, Gower Press, 1987

Chapter 9 – Action sequencing

No recommendations

Chapter 10 – Project management techniques
BEE R *and* F. *Project Management: The people challenge*. London, Institute of Personnel and Development, 1997

Chapter 11 – Experimenting
NOLAN V. *Open to Change*. MCB Publications, 1981, p 14–34
PETERS T *and* WATERMAN R. 'Experimenting organisations', in *In Search of Excellence*. London, Harper and Row, 1982, pp 134–150

Chapter 12 – Participative decision-making
NEUMANN J. *Enhancing Willingness to Participate*. Publication No. 811182, Vol. 49–04A. University Microfilms International, Ann Arbor, Michigan, 1988
GUEST D *and* Knight K (eds). *Putting Participation into Practice*. Aldershot, Gower Press, 1979
GILLIES E. *Employee Participation and Decision Making Structures*. Australian Government Publishing Service, Canberra, 1983
GILBERT J. 'Human factors – the key to getting a competitive edge', *Human Participation*, winter 1986/7
Priority Decision System (PDS): supplied by Work Science Associates, 26 Southwood Lawn Road, London N6 5SF
WATERMAN R Jr. *The Renewal Factor*. London, Bantam Press, 1988, p 84–90

Chapter 13 – Outside agents
KAKABADSE A. *How to Use Consultants*. MCB Press, Vol 4, no 1, 1983
Seeking Help From Management Consultants by Cabinet Office (Management and Personnel Office), 1985

Chapter 14 – Tracking
WARMINGTON *et al*. 'The evaluation of success in change', in *Organisation Behaviour and Performance: An open systems approach to change*, pp 188–194
PORRAS J. *Stream Analysis*. Reading, MA, Addison-Wesley, OD Series, 1987

Chapter 15 – Force-field analysis
FORDYCE J R *and* WELLS R. *Managing With People*. Reading, MA, Addison-Wesley, pp 106–8
PAGE D *and* JONES L. *Planned Change through Force Field Analysis*. Castlevale Ltd, 3 Station Parade, Balham SW12 9AZ

Chapter 16 – Other facilitation tools
WALTERS M. *Employee Attitude and Opinion Surveys*. London, Institute of Personnel and Development, 1996

WALTERS M. *Building the Responsive Organisation.* Maidenhead, McGraw-Hill, 1994

Chapter 17 – Sensing and surveys

FORDYCE J R *and* WELLS R. *Managing With People.* Reading, MA, Addison-Wesley, pp 143–146

JONES E J. 'The sensing interview', in *The 1973 Annual Handbook for Group Facilitators,* University Associates, California, pp 213–224

PLANT R. *Managing Change and Making It Stick.* Fontana, 1987, pp 66–72

Chapter 18 – Management by walking about

HALBERSTAM D. *The Reckoning.* London, Bloomsbury Publishing, 1986, p 209

PETERS T *and* WATERMAN R Jr. 'Experimenting organisations', in *In Search of Excellence,* London, Harper and Row, 1982

Chapter 19 – Team-building

BELBIN M. *Management Teams: Why they succeed or fail.* Oxford, Heinemann, 1981

GAWLINSKI G. *Planning Together: The art of effective teamwork.* London, Bedford Square Press, 1988

WOODCOCK M. *Team Development Manual.* Aldershot, Gower Publishing, 1979

WOODCOCK M and FRANCIS D. *Organisation Development through Team Building.* Aldershot, Gower Publishing, 1981

WATERMAN R Jr. *The Renewal Factor.* London, Bantam Press, 1988, pp 179–183; 207–212

Chapter 20 – Verbal skills

NOLAN V. *Open to Change.* MCB Publications, 1981, pp 59–61, 65

TORRINGTON D. *Face to Face in Management.* Hemel Hempstead, Prentice Hall International Inc, 1982

BLACK K. *Assertiveness at Work.* Maidenhead, McGraw-Hill, 1982

NELSON-JONES R. *Human Relationship Skills.* London, Cassell Educational Ltd, East Sussex, 1986, pp 106–162; 221–248

PEASE A. *Body Language.* New York, Sheldon Press, 1986

MARGERISON C. *Conversational Control for Managers.* London, Mercury Books Division, W H Allen and Co, 1987

Index